FABIO'S
Italian KITCHEN

FABIO VIVIANI

with MELANIE REHAK

HYPERION

NEW YORK

FABIO'S Italian KITCHEN

Library of Congress Cataloging-in-Publication Data has been applied for.

ISBN: 978-1-4013-1277-0

Photographs by Matt Armendariz
Prop styling by Robin Tucker
Photographs on pp. 137 and 240 courtesy of Yahoo!/*Chow Ciao! with Fabio Viviani*

Book design by Shubhani Sarkar

First Edition

10   9   8   7   6   5   4   3   2

THIS LABEL APPLIES TO TEXT STOCK

We try to produce the most beautiful books possible, and we are also extremely concerned about the impact of our manufacturing process on the forests of the world and the environment as a whole. Accordingly, we've made sure that all of the paper we use has been certified as coming from forests that are managed, to ensure the protection of the people and wildlife dependent upon them.

TO all my grandmas, Claudia and Gabriella and Maria. I miss you. Thank you for setting the bar so high for what an awesome family looks like.

TO my mom, as an "I'm sorry" for everything I did to you, and thank you for being so amazing to me.

TO Mike, Linda, Jimmy, and Danny Langner for reminding me every day what family is all about. Thank you for letting me in. I love you guys.

CONTENTS

My food is meant to be made and eaten. That's it. It's not meant to impress, it's meant to feed people.

One of the first things I learned to cook was an apple sponge cake. My great-grandma taught me how to do it after I set her on fire, when I was five and she was eighty-seven. I'll tell you the fire story later in this book. I have a lot of stories—some funny and some that still make me cry today. Some will inspire you. Some will make people say, "I will never have kids." But first, one other story about the apple cake: I once baked it for the Pope.

I had a lot of health problems as a kid. So when I was seven years old, my grandfather decided it would be a good idea to take me to Rome and get me blessed. I refused to leave the house without making not just one but two of these apple cakes, which my family called Fabio's Cake, for the Pope. We arrived in the waiting room at the Vatican two hours ahead of time, and in those two hours, I got so bored I ate one whole cake by myself. The other thing I did to pass the time was yell a lot, very loudly. Seeing that I was causing trouble, various Cardinals came over to say hello and try to calm me down. When they bent down to talk to me, I tried to knock off their hats. My mom was not so happy about either the yelling or the hats.

By the time the blessing mass finally started, I was out of patience, and as soon as I saw the Pope I started to scream as loud as I could, "I

have a cake for you!" Seeing all the chaos, the Pope came over to me and for ten whole minutes—longer than my family had ever seen before—I behaved. I gave him the cake, he gave me a hug and a blessing, and then, to thank him, I jumped up and yelled "*Tu hai un bel cappello!*" which basically means "Nice hat, dude!" Then I tried to whack off his tall ceremonial hat. Somehow he managed to hold it on with one hand while holding my cake in the other, and my parents got me out of there fast.

What can I say? That's the kind of kid I was. I come from a passionate family—after all, we're Italian. And a big part of being a passionate Italian is being passionate about food. It doesn't matter where you're from in Italy. It doesn't matter if you're a lawyer or a janitor: Food is your passion! My family has some very hardworking people, and my family has some lazy people, but all of them are crazy about food. The funny part is that they're passionate about something that we never really had. We were very poor and we didn't always have enough to eat, but it didn't matter: Even just a piece of bread on the family table was a gigantic celebration.

Just because we didn't have much didn't mean we had no tradition. I learned at a very young age that where food is concerned, things have to be done in a certain way. For example, in my family, roasted chicken is made with rose-

mary, sage, and garlic. If you have a chicken and you have sage and you have garlic but there is no rosemary around, then you can't do a roasted chicken! You have to do something else and everybody knows it. It's tradition, and people get very animated about it.

So for me, this isn't just a cookbook. I mean, it *is* a cookbook, otherwise you'll say, "Fabio, you're crazy! It's a cookbook!" But it's also twenty-six years of things that happened in my house that mostly revolved around food. It's a celebration of the biggest part of my life so far—my family. If you want to get a really great meal in Italy, you have to go to somebody's house. Once you're there, you're going to experience amazing food made with simple ingredients. So one of the

things I emphasize in this book is getting back to basics and enjoying little things—the small pleasures. It's incredible what you can do with an apple or an egg, for example, and tomato sauce is just tomatoes, olive oil, and garlic. That's it. There is no bacon. There is no onion. It's three ingredients that match perfectly, old world and old school.

This is how I cook in my own home, for comfort through the day and so that everybody who

comes there feels welcome. I make the dishes in this book, respecting Italian tradition, and I try very hard not to get too caught up in new kitchen technology.

That's also why you'll be able to cook 100 percent of the recipes in this book in your own kitchen. Actually, there are two reasons: First, because I say so; and second, because my food is not pretentious. My food is not complicated. My food is meant to be made and eaten. That's it. It's not meant to impress, it's meant to feed people. I'm not putting this book in front of you because I want you to become a three-star chef. I just want to make sure that when you're done cooking, every person you know will say, "That's a great freaking dish. Delicious! I wish I knew how to do it."

Having said that, please understand that this is not a book of Five-Minute Fixes by Fabio. Some of the dishes take some time, and you'll want to pour a glass of wine and a take deep breath before you make them. They aren't hard, but you have to create momentum around these recipes. If something needs to braise for three hours, go on with your life while it's cooking! Do the laundry, get another glass of wine, chase your dog, plant some tomatoes. It's not going to cook faster if you look at it. If you want to be lazy, avoid those recipes—you still have about 140 to choose from. But remember: There are people, maybe even people in your family, who enjoy braising something for six hours (and will probably also keep you company while you cook).

I hope you really enjoy these recipes. And as you're sipping a fantastic soup or deciding to make a risotto or pasta the way my grandmother made it, think about me as a little Italian boy everyone called Fabiolino, eating these

same dishes as I struggled and learned and grew up. The way my family cooks is not the only way, of course, but it's the only way *we* do it. For me, sharing these memories and recipes is like reconnecting to my family in Italy. I am so happy to bring you together with them around the table.

> *If you want to get a really great meal in Italy, you have to go to somebody's house.*

PS: Common sense always applies in the kitchen. Yes! Developing smart associations will help you a lot more than just following recipes precisely, so try to train your common sense as you cook. If you taste something you're cooking and you think it is missing salt, but you already added the pinch of salt I said you need, add another one! I won't come kidnap your pets in the night!

Another example: I often say pasta should be cooked in salted boiling water. What I mean by salted boiling water is about a gallon of water and a handful of salt. Now, I would like to make a speech about a handful: If you have a hand that is big like a sumo wrestler's head, then maybe you need only half a handful of salt. But if you have the hand of a three-year-old baby, then you

probably need two handfuls of salt. See what I mean? (For the record, a handful of salt is usually about two to three tablespoons.)

And caramelization: When chefs say to cook something "until caramelized, about 15 minutes," they're thinking about *their* stove, *their* fire, *their* pots and pans. At your house, you need to cook it until it *looks* caramelized. That's why you're much better off understanding what "caramelized" means rather than walking away for fifteen minutes and coming back to disaster. Caramelized is when you can see color. Vegetables release water, and you'll see that, too, in the form of a very light steam all over the veggies. Then they'll start to look translucent. Caramelized is the next step after that. All the moisture has disappeared, the vegetables will start to brown lightly on the edges, and the bottom of the pan has little brown bits here and there. In order to caramelize, vegetables have to touch the pan and the oil, so when you use a wider sauté pan, caramelizing takes less time than when you use a taller pot with a smaller-diameter bottom. I don't know how long it's going to take in your pan, because I don't know what pan you have! Welcome to common sense.

If you taste something you're cooking and you think it is missing salt, but you already added the pinch of salt I said you need, add another one! I won't come kidnap your pets in the night!

ON RECIPE BASICS IN THIS BOOK

- When I say "olive oil," you can use either regular olive oil or light olive oil at your discretion. But I strongly recommend using light olive oil for any cooking that involves high heat, like sautéing, frying, or roasting. Extra-virgin olive oil, which has a peppery, delicious taste, should only be used for drizzling, finishing, dressing salads, and other places where you want a strong olive flavor or are not cooking it for long, like in a quick pasta sauce. In Italy you'll never see somebody waste extra-virgin olive oil on cooking meat sauce. In the recipes where I think you should use extra-virgin olive oil, it's listed in the ingredients.
- When I say "salt and pepper," it's always kosher salt and freshly ground black pepper unless otherwise specified.
- When I say "butter," it's always unsalted butter unless otherwise specified.
- When I say "Parmesan," I mean imported Parmigiano-Reggiano from Italy, which is what I use. Or, if you want a less expensive alternative, get a good local American Parmesan cheese.
- When I ask for eggs (or egg yolks or whites), always try to use organic or free-range if possible, and always use large eggs.
- When I ask for parsley, it's always Italian flat parsley.

ON KITCHEN GEAR

Let's talk about utensils for a second. Everything on this list is something you can use in making at least one of the recipes in this book. But even if you don't have all of these things, you'll still be able to make most of the recipes. After all, we didn't have any fancy gadgets when I was a kid, and somehow we made all of them. Think of these as suggestions rather than requirements.

Electricals

Food processor
Ice cream maker
Stand mixer or handheld electric mixer
Stick blender

Pots and Pans

Baking sheet / sheet pan
10-inch cake pan
Dutch ovens or heavy casseroles with lids
    (medium and large)
Rectangular Pyrex or other baking dishes
    (6 × 9-inch and one other, larger size)
Saucepans (small, medium, large)
Sauté pans (small, medium, large)
Deep sauté pan
Ceramic nonstick sauté pan
10-inch and 9-inch round springform pans
Stockpots (large, extra large)

Knives

2 chef's knives, one big for chopping, one
    smaller for dicing

Small, sturdy boning/filleting knife

Small flexible knife for cleaning fish and cutting
    very thin slices

A few paring knives

7–8-inch Santoku knife

Serrated knife

Miscellaneous Items

Butcher's twine

Candy thermometer

Cheese grater

Cheesecloth

Colander

2-inch round cookie cutter

Cookie mat

Cutting boards

Ice cream scoop

Ladle

Mandoline

Meat mallet

Meat thermometer

Melon baller

Mesh strainer

Metal and glass mixing bowls (various sizes)

Microplane

Mortar and pestle

Pizza cutter

Plastic spatula

Potato masher

Potato ricer

Rolling pin

6-inch wooden skewers

Slotted spoon

Tongs

Whisk

Wire rack for cooling

Wooden spoons

ON MY PANTRY AND YOURS

The pantry is your in-house supermarket. When
you're missing something on your kitchen counter for your recipe, you go to the pantry. In my
house it was never very full, but we always
had the things we needed to make a few good
dishes. No boil-in bags, no packaged stuff, no
canned spaghetti—stuff to make food prepara-
tion easier, not to make prepared food. That's
the whole principle behind my family recipes,
but you have to have a well-stocked pantry. In
my house the pantry was like the secret weapon.
Every time you opened it, there was something
there you could use. You have to take care of
your pantry, though; an unstocked pantry is a
disaster. And don't confuse storage space with a
pantry. A pantry is for food, storage space is for
your socks, your shoes, your cat food, your toilet
paper. I don't want to go looking for cannellini
beans and end up with a roll of toilet paper in
my hand. A pantry is a lifestyle, so embrace it.
Here's what I like to keep in mine.

Anchovies

Arborio rice (for risotto)

Artichoke hearts

Baking powder

Baking soda

Balsamic vinegar

Canned beans

Dry beans (borlotti, cannellini, pigeon)

Breadcrumbs (for frying, coating, and using in
   meatballs and meat loaf)

Capers (for a quick sauce with lemon)

Dried chilies

Chocolate (it's always good to have chocolate)

Cinnamon sticks

Canned clams

All-purpose flour

Bread flour

Chestnut flour

Chickpea flour

Semolina flour

Whole wheat flour

Gelatin powder

Graham crackers

Various dried herbs and spices (rosemary,
   oregano, thyme, bay leaves, basil, sage, red
   pepper flakes, whole black peppercorns,
   whole and ground nutmeg, fennel seeds,
   mustard seeds, mustard powder, paprika and
   smoked paprika, saffron, ground cinnamon,
   ground white pepper, whole cloves, garlic
   salt, onion powder, celery salt, juniper
   berries)

Honey

Kosher salt (for texture)

Dried mushrooms (such as porcini or
   shiitake—for grinding into powder to add
   flavor to stocks or soups)

Mustard (grainy, yellow, and Dijon)

Nuts (hazelnuts, pine nuts, walnuts, any other
   nuts you love—great for pesto and other
   recipes)

Extra-virgin olive oil

Light olive oil

Regular/Classic olive oil

Green olives and black olives (your refrigerator
   can be part of your pantry, too!)

Orzo

Pasta shapes (some long, some short)

Polenta

Red wine vinegar

Kosher salt

Table salt (mostly for salting pasta water)

Sugar

Brown sugar

Powdered sugar

Canned or boxed tomatoes

Tomato paste

Tomato purée

Vanilla (extract and pods)

Vegetable oil (peanut or soybean)

Wild rice

Wine (preferably red, and it should be the kind
   you can drink)

Dry yeast packets

A pantry is for food. . . . I don't want to go looking for cannellini beans and end up with a roll of toilet paper in my hand.

BABY STEPS

Primi Passi

I have done so many things for the first time, from counting to three to counting to a thousand, from riding a bike to driving a car, from making a friend to finding a girlfriend. With dinner, you have the first glass of wine, then the first bottle. You kiss, you make love. You get your first gelato, then you *make* your first gelato. These are first steps—baby steps. *Primi passi.*

Everything that you experience in life will feature a primi passi section, but these primi passi are the basis for cooking. They are the foundation of this book. They will boost your morale and build your culinary backbone. You're going to master and then use these primi passi through the whole book.

Italian food is very simple, so our first steps are not going to be hard. The problem many people have is they set their sights too high at the beginning. If you've never run, you don't want to start by running a 5K. Just run around the block. Run around the park. Then run around your neighborhood. Then run around your neighborhood twice. Then, when your next-door neighbor is wondering what you're doing every morning running around the neighborhood, run a 5K. You have to acquire expertise by accomplishing very little things, and primi passi are those tiny things, those little moments of joy—the chopping, the searing, the roasting. Never underestimate the power of basic.

By the time you have completed the whole primi passi section successfully, you're gonna feel like the chef is in the house. Of course, if these recipes are things you already know how to do, move on! They'll always be here for you, just like they are for me.

FRESH EGG PASTA DOUGH

Pasta Fresca

I grew up with fresh egg pasta. The way my great-grandma kept me from destroying the household was to have me crack eight eggs on a cutting board and hand mix them with flour for hours. It's a very time-consuming maneuver! I am all about preserving tradition, but what about improving the execution of tradition so you can have traditional flavor in a tenth of the time? That's the way I teach people to make pasta. By following my way, anyone can make it. All you need is a food processor and a blade attachment.

10 egg yolks
Pinch of table salt
½ tsp. ground black pepper
2 tsp. olive oil
2 cups flour

TIP: Remember—even though I always ask for large eggs, egg sizes vary. If you see that after you put in the egg yolks, your pasta is sticky, add more flour, 1 tablespoon at a time.

Place the egg yolks in a food processor with the blade attachment, add the salt, pepper, and olive oil, and pulse a few times.

Add half of the flour and pulse until the eggs absorb it and you have a semi-thick paste. Add the rest of the flour and allow the blade to rotate continuously. When the dough is ready, you should see a ball-shaped mass of flour and eggs bouncing around the canister. If the dough is still too wet to the touch, add an extra tablespoon of flour. If it is a bit dry, add a little water as needed.

Take the pasta out and roll/shape according to the directions of the recipe you are making. If you're saving it for later, wrap it in plastic wrap and place it in the fridge for up to 6 days. (But pasta, according to my grandpa, must be consumed right away, or you should just make a risotto instead!)

Risotto   Serves 6

People don't do risotto, because they believe you have to sit there and stir for hours and hours and hours. Guys, get off your ass! So you have to go to the stove and stir every five minutes. Come on, that's a basic skill! If you cannot make circles with your hand and a wooden spoon, you don't deserve to eat risotto.

Heat the stock to a low boil.

Put the olive oil and the dollop of butter into a separate pan over low heat, add the onion, and cook very slowly for about 15 minutes *without* letting it caramelize. When the onions have softened, add the rice and turn up the heat to medium.

The rice will now begin to lightly fry, so keep stirring it. After a minute it will look slightly translucent. Add the wine and keep stirring until the rice has absorbed the wine. Then add your first ladle of hot stock, a good pinch of salt and a dash of pepper.

Turn the heat down to a simmer so the rice doesn't cook too quickly on the outside. Keep adding stock one ladle at a time, stirring and reducing at the same time over medium-low heat, allowing each addition of stock to be absorbed before adding the next. It will take around 15–20 minutes to add all the stock.

Remove from the heat and add the 5 tablespoons of butter and the Parmesan. Stir well. Let the risotto sit for a few minutes before you serve it.

> *If you cannot make circles with your hand and a wooden spoon, you don't deserve to eat risotto.*

4 cups vegetable stock
  (see recipe on page 264)
2 tbsp. olive oil
5 tbsp. butter, plus a dollop
  (about 1 tbsp.) more
1 large onion, finely chopped
2 cups Arborio rice
2 wine glasses of dry white
  wine
Salt and pepper
5 tbsp. butter
½ cup Parmesan cheese,
  grated

NOTE: The stirring process can be cut almost in half if you have a good nonstick pan. Be careful: some nonstick pans with black coating will release chemicals if heated for too long, so if you want to use nonstick, use a ceramic pan. Risotto also cooks well in a copper pan, which requires more stirring, but conducts heat better.

POTATO-RICOTTA GNOCCHI

Gnocchi di Patate e Ricotta

Serves 6

Gnocchi for a chef is bragging rights. You go anywhere and the chef is like, "Oh, I make the best gnocchi in town." Guys, get over it. The best gnocchi is my grandma's gnocchi. It's like a small pillow from heaven that's going to burst in your mouth. You will probably cry once you try my grandma's gnocchi. Make sure you plan ahead to make these the day before so the potato mixture can cool overnight.

Preheat the oven to 425°F.

Bake the potatoes for an hour until they are crispy on the outside and fluffy on the inside. Cool for a couple of hours, remove the insides with a spoon, and mash them, using a potato ricer or a fork, until they are very smooth.

Place the potatoes in a bowl and add the nutmeg, the salt, a pinch of pepper, the egg yolk, and the ricotta. Mix together to combine and let rest overnight in the refrigerator, uncovered.

The next day, spread the semolina flour in an even layer on a baking sheet or tray.

Then place the potato mixture in the bowl of a stand mixer and, using the paddle attachment, add the flour on low–medium speed. Once the mixture has come together, remove it from the bowl and cut it into fist-size balls.

Roll each ball in the palms of your hands and then form it into a cigar shape. Cut each of these tubes into 1-inch pieces. Place them on the bed of semolina flour on your tray and put the tray in the fridge for 10–20 minutes to set.

To cook the gnocchi, drop them into salted boiling water. When the first few rise to the top of the pot, remove all the gnocchi with a slotted spoon.

6 medium potatoes (russet or any other baking potato)

1½ a whole nutmeg, grated

1 tbsp. salt, plus pepper to taste

1 egg yolk

1 cup ricotta cheese

1 cup semolina flour

2 cups flour

NOTE: The potatoes have to be cold. Hot potatoes create steam, steam absorbs flour, and flour makes gnocchi chewy. Hello! Cold potatoes will absorb just enough flour for you to be able to cut and shape them.

SEMOLINA GNOCCHI

Gnocchi di Semola

Serves 4–6

The inside of these gnocchi will be lava-hot when they come out of the oven. Wait to eat them or just like my grandpa you will curse your lungs out because your tongue is blistering and you are in great pain. The best way to make them is by not planning to make them. Do it the next day when you have leftover polenta.

Preheat the oven to 375°F.

Heat the milk, cream or water, salt, and pepper in a saucepan over medium heat.

When it starts to simmer, add the semolina flour, stirring constantly with a whisk to make sure lumps do not form. Continue to whisk for 10 more minutes over low heat until the batter has become thick. Remove from heat and whisk in the eggs, half of the Parmesan, and the butter.

Pour into a sheet pan or onto a large wooden cutting board, making sure that the thickness is about ⅔ inch overall. Let it cool down completely. Once it is firm, cut the semolina into gnocchi using the mouth of a water glass or a 2-inch round cookie cutter.

Butter a baking dish, place the gnocchi in it in a single layer (it's fine if they overlap a little), and sprinkle them with the breadcrumbs and the rest of the Parmesan. Bake until golden brown, about 7–10 minutes. Serve with Brown Butter Sage Sauce (see recipe on page 20)

1 quart whole milk

1 cup heavy cream (for richer texture) or water (for lighter texture)

3 tsp. salt

1 tsp. pepper

1⅓ cups semolina flour

2 large eggs

2 cups Parmesan cheese, finely grated, divided in half

1 tbsp. butter, plus more for buttering the baking dish

½ cup breadcrumbs

TIP: Be like my grandma! For cutting out the gnocchi, wet the top of the polenta sheet with water to keep the glass or cookie cutter from sticking.

GRANDMA'S POLENTA

Polenta della Nonna

Serves 4 as an entrée or 8 as an appetizer

Butter, Parmesan, fancy cheese, truffles . . . that's all great. But you can have a delicious polenta with a pinch of salt, boiling water, and a bunch of fresh herbs. It's the ultimate cheap peasant food. We had a big wooden kitchen table and we used to serve the polenta right off the table in a gigantic pile. No dish, nothing. A nice way for you to serve this would be on a slab of marble in the middle of your table.

Bring the milk and water to a boil in a large pot. Add the semolina flour or polenta and whisk until it becomes thicker but is still creamy, about 15–20 minutes.

Beat the egg yolks in a bowl with a little water, then add them to the semolina mixture along with the Parmesan and salt and pepper to taste. Stir and remove from heat.

In a sauté pan, cook the rosemary in the butter for about 5 minutes over medium heat, then mix it into the polenta.

Serve creamy or let it cool down. The more it cools down, the firmer it will become. You can also let it sit in the fridge overnight on a flat sheet pan and the next day cut squares and fry them in oil for a great treat.

1 quart milk

1 quart water

2½ cups semolina flour or polenta

5 egg yolks

3 cups Parmesan cheese, grated

Salt and pepper

1 tbsp. rosemary, finely chopped

8 tbsp. (one stick) butter

TIP: Flavor the polenta with whatever soft cheese you like or have left over. Grandma won't be too upset.

NOTE: Semolina flour and polenta are both made of corn. The only difference is that semolina is more finely ground, which will give you a smoother consistency than the coarser, more traditional polenta. It's like the difference between steel-cut oatmeal and regular oatmeal.

CHUNKY BASIL PESTO

Pesto

Anyone with at least one finger can make pesto, and if for some reason you're not equipped with fingers, you can press the food processor button with your elbow. That's how easy this is. If you want to season a pasta, add a bit more oil so it's more liquid. If you want to use it as a topping or a spread, make it nice and thick. And if you have a date, ease up on the garlic.

In a food processor, combine the basil leaves, olive oil, pine nuts, garlic, salt, and pepper and process until just mixed but still chunky.

Add the Parmesan or Romano and pulse to combine. *Do not over-process.* Store in the fridge in an airtight container or jar, topped with a layer of olive oil.

3–4 cups basil leaves, packed
2 cups extra-virgin olive oil
1 cup pine nuts
5 cloves garlic
Salt and pepper
1½ cups Parmesan cheese or Romano cheese, grated

Anyone with at least one finger can make pesto, and if for some reason you're not equipped with fingers, you can press the food processor button with your elbow.

FABIO'S TOMATO SAUCE WITH OIL AND GARLIC

Pomarola

Makes 2 cups

This is the simplest of sauces out there, so simple I don't even feel I want to call it cooking. But it's also delicious, so it does deserve the name of sauce.

Smash the garlic with the back of a knife. Place the garlic and 5 tablespoons of olive oil in a saucepan and cook over medium heat until the garlic is golden brown. Add the tomatoes and generous pinches of salt and pepper.

Cook over medium-high heat until the sauce is thick and no longer watery, about 10–15 minutes. Add the remaining 3 tablespoons of olive oil and turn the heat to high. Stir, crushing the tomatoes with the back of a wooden spoon. Cook until the oil turns red, then turn off the heat and add the basil at the very end.

6 cloves garlic
8 tbsp. extra-virgin olive oil
1 28-oz. can of whole plum tomatoes (packed only in tomato juice)
Salt and pepper
10 basil leaves

TIP: Make 3 times the Pomarola you need and freeze the extra in Ziploc bags. It will last up to 6 months.

BROWN BUTTER SAGE SAUCE

Burro Bruno e Salvia

Italy is not about the fuss, it's all about the flavor. When you brown butter slow and low, the protein in the butter goes to the bottom of the pan and starts to caramelize and create a nutty, intense popcorn flavor. The addition of the sage is just a step beyond—because we like to go bold and big before we go home. This is a great drizzle for any pasta or gnocchi, and a fantastic topping for steak or fish.

Put the butter and the sage in a large sauté pan over low heat and cook until the foaming subsides. The sauce should be golden brown in color and the sage leaves will be nice and crispy.

Season to taste with salt and pepper. If the sauce looks separated or too oily, add a bit of warm water; if it looks too watery, keep it on the heat and reduce for a few minutes until it thickens.

½ lb. (2 sticks) butter
1 cup fresh sage leaves
   (about 12–14)
Salt and pepper

CAPER SAUCE WITH BURNT LEMON

Capperi e Limone

This is great on chicken dishes (see my recipe for Chicken Piccata on page 178), and you can also use it on fish. It's very sour and a little salty. It also adds pizazz to vegetable dishes. Make some roasted or grilled vegetables and drizzle it on top—it's amazing. It will keep for about a week, but why would you make it and let it sit there for so long?

Flour the lemon slices. Put the oil and lemon slices in a hot pan over medium heat and cook until the lemons are caramelized and nicely browned on all sides. The flour will stick to the bottom of the pan a bit (but it's all good).

   Add the garlic and the capers, then deglaze the pan with the stock, scraping the bottom to release any flour bits. Reduce the sauce over medium heat until it has thickened a little and has a denser consistency. Add the butter at the end to make the sauce smoother, and season with salt and pepper to taste.

1 whole lemon, sliced into 10 rounds
½ cup unbleached flour
2 tbsp. olive oil
1 clove garlic, minced
½ cup capers packed in water, drained
1½ cups chicken stock (see recipe on page 260)
1 tbsp. butter
Salt and pepper

TIP: When you cook a sauce or meat, you get little caramelized brown bits and drippings stuck to the bottom of the pan. These have a lot of flavor, so when you deglaze, add wine, stock, or some other liquid to get them off the bottom of the pan and back into the dish.

GRANDMA'S MEAT SAUCE

Sugo di Carne della Nonna

Makes 2–3 quarts

The original of this sauce comes from the city of Bologna in northern Italy. For hardcore flavor, you can replace a quarter of the meat with mortadella. If you have the time, I beg you to make this recipe with the heat on low. It will take six to eight hours, but you will double the flavor.

Heat a large saucepan over medium-high heat and add the olive oil. When it has heated up, add the celery, carrots, onion, rosemary, and sage and cook until caramelized, about 15 minutes. Add the garlic, cook for 2–3 minutes more, then deglaze the pan (see page 21 for a tip on deglazing) with white wine and reduce until the pan is almost dry.

Add the ground beef and cook, breaking it into small pieces, until no traces of pink remain. Add the red wine and reduce until it has disappeared. Add the tomato sauce and then the tomato paste, and reduce until the sauce is thick and rich. If you prefer to cook the sauce faster, turn the heat to medium-high and make sure to stir freqently to prevent the sauce from burning at the bottom of the pan. It will take about 2 hours this way.

Season with salt and pepper to taste. Serve over pasta. Something long like fettuccine or spaghetti works well, but anything is fine. (See note on pasta/sauce pairs on page 83.)

3 tbsp. olive oil

2 cups celery, diced

2 cups carrots, diced

2 cups onion, diced

1 sprig rosemary

1 sprig sage

5 cloves garlic, smashed

1 cup white wine

2 lb. ground beef

2 cups red wine

2 cups Fabio's Tomato Sauce (see recipe on page 18)

1 cup tomato paste

Salt and pepper

TIP: For a perfect meat sauce, don't use ultra-lean meat; a little fattier meat means more *flavor*!

HOMEMADE RICOTTA

Ricotta della Mamma

Bring the milk to a boil in a large saucepan, letting it reach 181°F. You will need a thermometer for this unless you're my grandma.

Turn off the heat, add the vinegar, the lemon juice, and the salt. As the milk begins to curdle, stir it with a whisk just a few times to mix in the lemon and the salt.

Cover and let the mixture cool down for about 2 hours. When it is cool, strain it through cheesecloth over a pot, pressing the curds with a wooden spoon to squeeze out the liquid. It will keep for 4–5 days in the fridge.

1 gallon whole milk

⅓ cup white wine vinegar

1 tbsp. lemon juice

A pinch of salt

TIP: For a creamier ricotta, substitute heavy cream for half the milk.

SUNDRIED TOMATOES

Pomodori Secchi

If you start making these at eleven o'clock at night, the next morning at six you'll have the best sundried tomatoes for breakfast that you ever had. Yes, for breakfast. Because they will smell so good that you cannot wait.

Put all ingredients into a metal bowl, mix well, and let rest for about 1 hour. The tomatoes will release more water.

Preheat the oven to 225°F.

Put a wire rack onto a sheet pan, then place the tomatoes on the rack cut side up. Roast for about 7 hours.

Store in olive oil in a mason jar in your fridge.

3 lb. Roma tomatoes, cut in half and seeds squeezed out

2 tbsp. olive oil

½ cup fresh thyme, chopped

1 tbsp. salt

1 tbsp. pepper

Limoni Dolci

When you roast citrus, you bring out the sweetness. Try some iced tea with caramelized lemon; make some vinaigrette dressing with it. From now on, every time you are going to use a raw lemon, unless you're using a slice in your water, try a roasted one instead.

Mix all the ingredients together in a bowl. Place the lemons open-face down on a really hot grill or in a hot sauté pan with a touch of olive oil or butter over medium to high heat.

Grill for about 10 minutes, moving the lemons around, until the open side is caramelized.

10 lemons, cut in half crosswise

2 tbsp. fresh thyme, chopped

Salt and pepper

2 tbsp. olive oil

Butter or olive oil for roasting (if using a pan rather than a grill)

OLIVE, ZUCCHINI, AND TOMATO BREAD TOPPING

Dadolata di Olive, Zucchine, e Pomodoro

Makes 6–10 appetizers

This recipe uses olives, zucchini, and tomatoes, but a good dadolata can be made from any other vegetables that are about to get too old to eat. It can be used as a topping for bread or served as a side.

Starting with the tomatoes, put the ingredients in a food processor with the blade attachment, pulsing each ingredient for about 20 1-second bursts before adding the next.

Serve over sliced bread or as a side dish.

30 small cherry tomatoes

2 whole zucchini, diced

1 cup green or black olives, pitted

1 cup extra-virgin olive oil

2 tbsp. balsamic glaze (see recipe on page 268)

1 tsp. pepper

1 tsp. salt

1 clove garlic

1 sprig thyme, leaves only

Juice of 1 lemon

CHERRY TOMATO SALAD WITH ORANGE, CUCUMBER, AND FETA

Arancie e Pomodori

If you want to add some spice, use a dash of white pepper, which won't clash with the orange.

Place the orange segments, tomatoes, cucumber, and feta in a bowl and mix well.

Add the basil, olive oil, and salt and mix well again. Serve.

3 oranges, peeled and cut into segments with the membranes removed (Some people call these supremes, but since I'm Italian, I don't use that French word.)

20 cherry tomatoes, cut in half

1 cucumber, diced

1 cup feta cheese, crumbled

30 basil leaves

4 tbsp. extra-virgin olive oil

A pinch of salt

GARLIC, ANCHOVY, AND CAPER DIP WITH RAW VEGETABLES

Bagna Cauda Fiorentina

Serves 4–6 as an appetizer

My family used this as a very basic dressing for salads of bitter greens like arugula, kale, or mustard greens. It's also good on these greens when you sauté them. When they're so bitter that you'd rather starve than eat them, bagna cauda is very handy.

Cook the garlic in boiling water for 5–6 minutes.

In a saucepan, combine the anchovies, the garlic cloves, and the oil and let them simmer over medium-low heat for about 20–30 minutes.

While the anchovy-garlic mixture is cooking, get the celery, fennel, and carrots ready to serve as dipping sticks. You can use them raw, or if you like more tender vegetables, you can blanch them in hot salted water for about 5 minutes, then rinse them off under cold water and pat dry.

When the dip has finished simmering, let it cool down a bit and add the parsley, salt, and pepper while it is still warm. Serve it in a bowl with the veggies on the side for dipping.

4 whole heads of garlic, peeled and broken into single cloves

7 anchovy fillets (rinsed if salted, or packed in vinegar)

1 cup extra-virgin olive oil

3 stalks celery, cut in half lengthwise

3 fennel bulbs, cores removed and cut into slices

3 carrots, peeled, tops removed, and sliced into sticks

3 sprigs parsley, finely chopped

Salt and pepper

NAKED RAVIOLI WITH RICOTTA AND SPINACH

Gnudi

Preheat the oven to 375°F.

Mix all the ingredients together in a large bowl. With an ice cream scoop, portion out 2-ounce balls (about the size of a tablespoon). Shape each ball into a football shape and place onto an ungreased cookie sheet.

Bake for approximately 10–15 minutes, until the outsides of the ravioli start to dry out and the tops start to brown.

Serve with Brown Butter Sage Sauce (see recipe on page 20) or, for a heartier dish, try Naked Ravioli with Fresh Tomato Sauce (see recipe on page 89).

2 lb. baby spinach, wilted and chopped (about 4 lbs. raw. To wilt, boil for about a minute and drain thoroughly.)

2 lb. ricotta cheese (see recipe on page 24)

1 cup Parmesan cheese, grated

2 tsp. salt

2 tsp. pepper

1 tsp. nutmeg, freshly grated if possible

1 egg

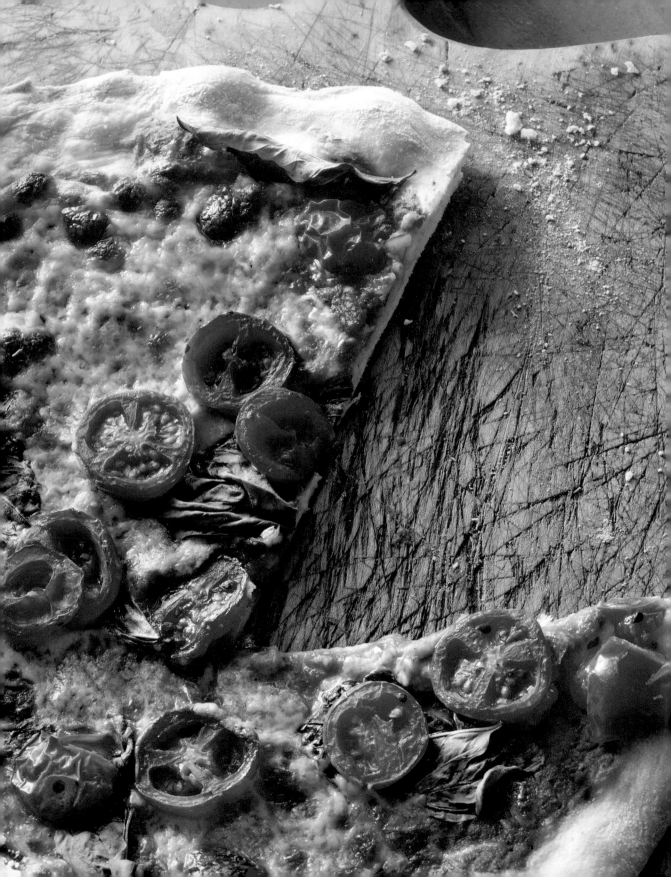

CLASSIC PIZZA

La Pizza

The south of Italy is famous for pizza, but it is not my region. My region is Tuscany. However, my mom's sister married this wonderful man from Naples in southern Italy, and he taught us how to make pizza. This is not my traditional family recipe—it's *his* family recipe, but who cares? It tastes good, so as a good Italian, I take ownership of it. This is a basic recipe, but you can put anything on top of a pizza pie. What would you like?

Preheat the oven to 400°F.

In a stand mixer with a hook attachment, mix the yeast, water, and sugar. Then add the flour in small amounts, mixing well between each addition.

When the dough is mixed well and not too sticky, use a little oil to help remove it from the bowl. Place the dough on a lightly floured surface, cover it with a dry linen towel, and let it rise for 30 minutes.

Roll out the dough, shape it, and transfer it to a sheet tray or pizza pan. Drizzle the dough with the olive oil, then spread the mozzarella evenly over the entire crust. Next, distribute the cherry tomatoes evenly, then the basil. Salt and pepper the pizza and bake for about 9–10 minutes, or until the crust is as crispy and the cheese as melted as you like them. Sprinkle with the Parmesan and serve.

For the dough:

1 packet (or ¼ oz.) dry active yeast

1½ cups warm water

1 tsp. sugar

4 cups flour, plus a few pinches for dusting

1 tbsp. extra-virgin olive oil

For the topping:

1 tbsp. extra-virgin olive oil

5 oz. mozzarella cheese, shredded

10 cherry tomatoes, cut in half

4 large basil leaves, cut into strips

Salt and pepper

2 tbsp. Parmesan cheese, grated

Additional toppings you can add before baking:

5 oz. prosciutto, thinly sliced

Chopped olives

Mushrooms

Onions

Anything you like!

My mom always tells me, "The good news about you is that you're alive. The bad news about you is that when you were born, you came out dead." My umbilical cord was wrapped around my neck, and I was stuck sideways. My heart had stopped beating, so the doctors did an emergency C-section. They pulled me out and massaged me, and luckily I came back to life and started breathing again. (Maybe God knew I was destined to someday meet the Pope!) So the other thing my mom says is: "You were dead already! Life is going to look up for you." The question for a long time was, "Will this kid be normal, since he was deprived of so much oxygen?" The answer, of course, is no, but not because of that!

I lived in my grandparents' apartment in a low-income complex in Florence. My parents, Renza and Valter, had me when they were just seventeen, so when I was born my father's parents were still taking care of my parents. In the apartment there was one regular bedroom, another small bedroom, and a kitchen in the living room. There was also a bathroom and a little balcony. My grandparents, Adriano and Claudia, got the bigger bedroom, and my mom and my dad had the smaller one. My great-grandmother Maria, who was in a wheelchair, lived with us, too, and she had no bedroom. But there was a small room—more like a closet—off the kitchen, where you could keep brooms and things, and

that was my great-grandma's bedroom. This room was so small that when you opened the door, it touched the bed. The bed fit in the room perfectly and at the end of it there was about three feet of empty space. That's it. So you could either stand in that space or be in the bed.

For me, there wasn't even a bed. When I was a baby, I had a crib in my parents' room at the end of their bed. As a little kid I spent a couple of years sleeping with my mom and dad. Then I got too big, so they moved me into the living room and my bed was a folding chair in the kitchen area. You know those beach chairs where you pull up the arms so you can lie flat? That was what I slept on, with only a thin cushion.

When I was four or five years old, my grandpa and I would go on Sunday nights to clean butcher

> *You only call it a struggle the minute you realize other people have it better. Since I didn't know that, for me it was just life and I thought life was great.*

shops, the vegetable guy's store, or the bottega, to earn some extra money. When my grandma was sixty-five and had to stop work, too, because she was too old to be employed, every night she worked as a cleaning lady for different stores in my neighborhood. She was paid in food—an extra piece of bread or a jar of Nutella or some scraps of meat. It was a constant struggle, but to me it didn't feel like a struggle because it was just what we did. You only call it a struggle the minute you realize other people have it better. Since I didn't know that, for me it was just life and I thought life was great.

But the diet on our table wasn't great: bread, flour, water, some tomato, eggs. It wasn't complete or very balanced. There was almost no meat or fish and there were very few vegetables besides what grew in my grandpa's garden on a small piece of land near our building. The result was that I was anemic and had a lot of illnesses related to my poor immune system, including a calcium deficiency that made my bones very fragile. My grandmother used to put rusty nails in water and make me drink the liquid to get some iron. She would also make chicken broth and blend it with the chicken bones into a pasty mixture, and I drank that for the calcium. The only real meal I got was at night.

> *Nutella was one of the few things that kept me under control. My mom would say, "If you don't sit down, I'm not getting the Nutella!" And I'd be petrified.*

I would complain sometimes about not getting my favorite foods all the time, of course. But my grandpa would always say, "Don't complain too much about what you're eating. When I was your age, I was eating potato skins." (He was a good man, but I called him the Mafioso Nonno because even though we never really knew how he earned a living, he could get anything done with one phone call. If someone we liked had their car stolen, he'd just pick up the phone and the next morning the car would reappear in the garage, washed and with a full tank of gas.) Once every few weeks he'd take me to the hospital to see kids who were having chemotherapy or were otherwise sick. We'd bring them cake or pie or something and spend half a day there, keeping them company. I never understood why at the time, but of course he did it to show me how lucky I was, so I would stop complaining about not getting enough Nutella.

I blame that addiction on my mom, who used to mix Nutella with milk and put it in my baby bottles to keep me quiet. Even when I was older, Nutella was one of the few things that kept me under control. My mom would say, "If you don't sit down, I'm not getting the Nutella!" And I'd be petrified.

As for real meals, eggs were the only thing that kept us going. My grandfather had a chicken coop on the land where his garden was. The chickens would lay fifty eggs a day, but my grandpa didn't come home until dinnertime, around 7:30 or 8:00, when he would bring the eggs. So the only full meal—eggs—was in the evening. Every night my grandma cooked eggs. Eggs with tomato. Eggs with eggs. Eggs with spinach. Eggs with eggs again. Half of them were made into a frittata, and half into what we call *occhio del bue*—bull's eye (the white and the yolk, over easy). Then . . . Sunday! Eggs with meatballs! There was never enough meat to have a steak. It was only because of Grandma's cleaning job at the butcher shop that we even had bits and pieces of meat. We ground everything and mixed it with bread and still more eggs. Then we'd shape it into balls—I call them meatballs now, but there wasn't enough meat to be a meatball, it was more like a bread ball—and braise them in marinara sauce. Sunday was amazing, not because the dinner was great but because it was not just eggs. It was something different. And that was enough.

APPETIZERS

Antipasto

CH. **02**

Antipasto in Italy is also like a catwalk: a procession of one little thing after the other.

In Italy, antipasto is something you eat regardless of what the meal is. You could have a five- or six-course meal planned and still have a gigantic amount of antipasto. You'd never say, "Hey, I'm not too hungry, I'm only getting a little antipasto," the way you'd order a small appetizer in America. It's not part of the meal—it's almost like foreplay.

Antipasto in Italy is also like a catwalk: a procession of one little thing after the other. It could be as simple as a piece of bread or bruschetta spread with olive oil, or it could be enough food for a full-on meal before the meal. It can be one thing or twenty different things, from olives to roasted peppers to cold cuts and chicken livers. You still eat it all.

The best thing about antipasto is that it gives the cook the chance to make a meal without having starving people hanging around asking what's for dinner, because there's stuff to eat already. Of course, in my family it didn't quite work that way. Whenever my mom would make something like fritters or meatballs for antipasto, everyone would eat them as she made the batches, so the first ten would be gone before she'd made the second ten. Then, when it was time to sit down at the table, she would put the platter down in the center and there would be just a few left of whatever she had made. My grandpa would look at her and say, "That's all you made?" And she would look at him and yell, "Give me a break! Get out of my kitchen!"

TOMATO TART

Torta al Pomodoro

Serves 6

To make the crust, put the flour and butter into a food processor with the blade attachment and incorporate the butter by pulsing a few times. Add the water 1 tablespoon at a time while continuing to pulse. When all the flour is absorbed, remove the dough from the food processor and work it with your hands a bit to form a ball. Cover it with a slightly moist linen towel and place it in the fridge till you need it.

Butter a 10-inch round springform pan. Roll out the dough on a floured surface to about ¼-inch thick. It should be large enough to completely cover the pan and hang over the sides. Using a fork, make holes all over the dough, then refrigerate for about 2 hours.

To make the filling, put the celery, carrots, onion, garlic, and tomatoes into a Dutch oven or a lidded nonstick pan over medium heat, drizzle them with the olive oil, and season with salt and pepper. Cook and reduce for about 1 hour, covered. Stir occasionally to make sure the tomatoes don't stick to the bottom of the pan.

Take the lid off and keep cooking, still over medium heat, for another 15 minutes, pressing the tomatoes with a potato masher until they are completely crushed and the mixture has reduced completely. Transfer it to a bowl to cool down. Once it has reached room temperature, place it in the fridge for about 30 minutes to chill.

To make the tart, preheat the oven to 375°F.

Pour the filling into the dough and cover it with the basil leaves. Fold the extra dough hanging over the side of the pan toward the center. All of the tomato filling should be covered except a small part in the middle. Bake for about 1 hour or until the crust is nice and brown and flaky.

Let it cool down, then run a knife around the edges of the pan to make sure that the pastry dough is detached from the sides. Remove the springform sides and serve the tart on the pan bottom at room temperature, sprinkled with flaky shaved Parmesan if you want.

For the crust:

2 cups plus 1 tbsp.
   unbleached flour

10 tbsp. butter, cold, plus
   more butter for the pan

5 tbsp. water, cold

For the filling:

2 medium celery stalks,
   chopped

2 carrots, diced

1 medium-size red onion,
   chopped

2 cloves garlic, minced

2 lb. very ripe tomatoes,
   cut in large pieces and
   pressed to drain (see
   note below)

3 tbsp. olive oil

Salt and pepper

1 bunch basil

Shaved Parmesan
   (optional)

TIP: To drain the tomatoes, cut them in half and squeeze in the palm of your hand, cut side down, toward the sink.

CHICKEN LIVER CROSTINI

Fegatini di Pollo

Makes about 2 cups of pâté

I remember challenging my grandpa to see who could get more pâté on a single finger. His fingers were very fat. I never won.

Heat the oil over medium heat in a large heavy-bottomed sauté pan. Add the shallots and garlic and cook, stirring, until the shallots have browned (about 10 minutes).

Salt and pepper the chicken livers and add them to the pan. Cook, stirring gently from time to time, for about 10 minutes, until they are cooked but still a bit pink in the center.

Add the brandy, turn the heat up to medium high, and cook until most of the brandy has evaporated, another 5–6 minutes. Remove from heat.

When the livers have cooled a bit, place the contents of the pan in a food processor with the blade attachment and add the capers, anchovies, and cream. Process until you have a chunky mixture, or a bit longer if you want a smoother pâté.

Serve on toasted bread.

6 tbsp. olive oil

3 shallots, very finely chopped

3 cloves garlic, crushed

Salt and pepper

1½ lb. chicken livers, trimmed, washed, and patted dry

⅔ cup brandy (use white wine for a tangier flavor)

1 cup capers, rinsed

½ cup salted anchovies, rinsed

3–4 tbsp. heavy cream

DEAD RICOTTA
IN THE GARDEN

Ricotta ni Prato

Serves however many you invite over, but you shouldn't invite anyone, it's so good. (But really it serves 4.)

Whatever is left over from your garden or is too little to make a salad can be used for the vegetable topping in this recipe. We had so few vegetables and herbs sometimes, my father used to joke and say, "Instead of picking them and bringing them into the kitchen, why don't we just toss the ricotta out the window into the back garden so we can get more?" That's why I call this "dead ricotta in the garden."

Mix the ricotta with the Pecorino, the flour, a good pinch of salt, and the egg yolks. When it is all well mixed, season it to taste with pepper.

In another bowl, mix the tomatoes, the basil, and the snap peas. Add the extra-virgin olive oil, a splash of vinegar, and some more salt, mix, and place in the fridge. Refrigerating the tomato mix provides a nice temperature contrast between the hot pancake and the cold vegetables when you assemble the dish.

Heat the olive oil in a nonstick pan over medium heat. Using an ice cream scoop, make balls of the ricotta mixture and place them in the hot oil. Use a plastic spatula to flatten each one a bit, so it looks like a lumpy disc.

Fry the ricotta cakes for a couple of minutes or until golden brown, then turn them over and fry them on the other side for one more minute.

Serve all the cakes at once, family style, with a good spoonful of the tomato-and-pea mixture and a drizzle of extra-virgin olive oil on top of each one.

1 lb. good crumbly ricotta cheese

2 tbsp. Pecorino cheese, grated

2 tbsp. flour

Salt and pepper

3 egg yolks

20 cherry tomatoes, cut in half and seeded

About 30 basil leaves, preferably small ones

A handful of snap peas, cut into small pieces

2 tbsp. extra-virgin olive oil

Red wine vinegar

4 tbsp. olive oil

RICOTTA-FILLED DATES WRAPPED IN PROSCIUTTO

Datteri

Serves 8–10 as an appetizer

Preheat the oven to 450°F.

Cut the dates in half and use a teaspoon to place a dollop of ricotta in each half.

Wrap each half-date in a half-slice of prosciutto and place them in a baking pan. Drizzle with extra-virgin olive oil and dust with pepper.

Bake for 10 minutes.

25 dried dates, as large as possible

1 lb. ricotta cheese

25 slices prosciutto, cut in half lengthwise

Extra-virgin olive oil

Pepper

Now I'm going to tell you why my family put me to work cooking for them at the age of five. As I said earlier, one of the first things I ever learned to make in the kitchen was an Italian (of course!) apple cake. (You can find the recipe on page 208).

Basically, I ended up learning this recipe because my grandfather used to keep gunpowder around the apartment for when he went hunting pheasant and wild boar. When I was five, I started secretly stealing bits of his gunpowder and collecting it in a little plastic bag. Fire and explosions fascinated me. I had some friends who had a television, and together we used to watch American imports dubbed in Italian. My favorite show was *The Dukes of Hazzard*. For me, that was the life—jumping into a car through the window, blowing things up, and shooting things.

One day, when I had enough gunpowder saved up, I made a paste from the gunpowder, some of the rubbing alcohol my diabetic grandma used for her insulin shots, and olive oil (I'd heard on television that if you mix gunpowder with oil, the fire burns more slowly). I spread it on the floor all around the couch. Then I climbed up on the couch and lit the paste, just for the fun of it.

So there I was, standing on the couch with this barricade of flames around me, yelling *"Victory!"* There was smoke everywhere. My great-grandma wheeled herself in and got the fiery paste on her wheels. She looked like a moving firework—screaming, lit up, rolling, screaming some more. She tried to grab me but couldn't because of the wheelchair. My dad was taking a shower, he heard me shouting *"Victory!"* and Great-grandma screaming, he saw thick smoke and had no idea what was going on. He thought the house was on fire. He got Great-grandma out of the wheelchair, her blanket half on fire, grabbed me by the T-shirt, and put the fire out.

My family and the next-door neighbors (who used to sometimes help look after me) had a summit at my kitchen table. No one could afford a babysitter, so all they could say was, "What are we going to do with this kid?" Great-grandma said, "I'll take care of him." Everyone said, "You're crazy! You can't take care of him. You can't even follow him—you're in a wheelchair!" But she was smart and she said, "I have an idea." She used to cook all day. She made bread, fresh pasta, and prepared the eggs for the evening meal. She told them, "This kid wants to play with fire"—we still had a wood stove—"I'll teach him how to cook." My mom was doubtful: "You'll never get him to stand still for more than ten minutes." But my great-grandma said, "I'll do it." And she did.

My great-grandma guided me through all the recipes she had. If I was out of control, she whacked me on the hand with a long wooden spoon; she had about three feet on me at any given time. She kept the spoon where a cop keeps a nightstick, and when Grandma was looking at me and she had her hand on the wooden spoon, I froze. But no matter what I did, she was never upset with me. She and my dad would argue about it, though, and she would beat my dad with the spoon if he yelled at me. My dad would say, "You can't hit him with a wooden spoon!" And she'd say, "You yell at him all the time when he misbehaves!" And then he'd yell, "Yelling is not hitting with a spoon!"

But mostly the spoon was for cooking. Great-grandma started by having me use it to make batters. Then she let me put wood in the stove and sauté things. Because of her wheelchair, she couldn't really reach the table, so she made fresh pasta from eggs and flour in an aluminum bowl on her lap. The pasta machine was at the edge of the table so she could roll out the dough.

She used me as an extension of her own body. I would stand on the wheelchair, waving a spoon like a cavalier's sword. Standing between her legs, I could reach the stove and the table, and as she wheeled around, I cooked for her. That's when she started to make things like chicken cacciatore, slightly more complicated recipes. She couldn't butcher a chicken, but I learned how to do that and much more as a five-, six- and seven-year-old. Because of my poor health, I missed a lot of school, so I spent a lot of time at home with Great-grandma, and together we cooked for six people every day.

She'd be in her wheelchair holding the bowl steady on the table and I'd stand on a chair mixing fresh pasta dough or apple cake with a spoon. I'd say, "Can I go play?" And she'd say, "You can't go play until there are no more lumps." I had a wooden spoon and I was five years old: There

were going to be lumps for three hours! But she really got hold of me and redirected my energy. I could have destroyed life and appliances and furniture in those three hours and instead I was just stirring a freaking cake.

And do you know how many hours I spent stirring polenta? Standing at the stove on the wheelchair, my grandmother holding the back of my shirt with one hand and the chair with the other, I stirred polenta with an old whisk for hours on end. Hours! Her face was so wrinkled up that you could barely see her eyes, but she saw everything. I'd say, "Grandma, I'm done." And without even looking at it she'd say, "It isn't done. That's not good. You have to do it more." And I'd say, "How can you even see?" And she would just repeat, "It can't be done. Do it more." She's the person who taught me to do it right or do it twice. For her it was all about doing it right the first time. After I set her on fire she said, "I'm eighty-seven and you're only five but there's got to be a way." She knew better. She found my soft spot and then I made a career out of it.

SOUPS

Zuppe e Brodetti | CH. 03

Anything you can eat with a spoon is a soup.

In Italy, soup is a big deal. Soups have the flavor and personality of the region they come from. In the south, you find a lot of starches, potatoes, beans, and spiciness. In the north, you find something lighter from a starch point of view, but heavier in meat and fish. In my house, soup was always made with whatever was available at that specific moment. If my mom came home with a basket of green veggies from the backyard, that's what went into the soup. If my aunt came for a visit with twenty pounds of beans, that's what went in. If my grandpa had shot a pheasant, it went in, and if we had meat, my mom made meatballs for Italian wedding soup (see recipe on page 64).

Anything you can eat with a spoon is a soup.

(And please do not eat risotto with a spoon! Don't you dare! If you cannot eat risotto with a fork, it's too loose. And if it's too loose, you don't have risotto, you have soup.) Soups in Italy are full-blown meals with texture. We don't drink soup, we eat soup. Cream of tomato soup? Lobster bisque? What? Give me a whole lobster diced and in fish broth and I'll call it a soup.

My mom would save soup in the freezer for months at a time, because in Italy, every ten minutes somebody shows up at your house and you want to feed them. So you give them soup because you can do it ahead and freeze it and no one will say anything. You can't freeze pasta or meat—those are taboos. But it's okay to freeze soup. Nobody's going to get upset about it.

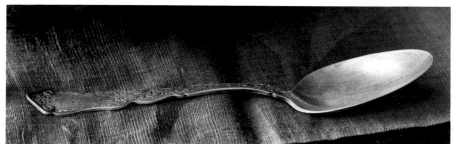

MY AUNT FROM SIENA'S BEAN SOUP

Zuppa della Zia di Siena   Serves 6–8

Place the beans in a pot with salted water and bring to a boil. Adjust to a medium boil and cook until the beans are tender, about 1 hour. Drain the beans, reserving the cooking liquid.

Heat the oil in a large nonstick sauté pan over medium heat, then add the pancetta and the sausage and cook until they start to brown. Add the onion and continue cooking for about 5 minutes, or until it has softened, then add the garlic and cook for another minute.

Pour in the wine to deglaze the pan, and cook to reduce slightly. (See page 21 for a tip on deglazing.) Add the beans and enough of the reserved bean-cooking liquid to cover everything, then add about another inch of liquid on top. Put a cover on the pan and let the beans simmer very gently for 10–15 minutes.

Stir in the parsley and adjust for salt and pepper. Transfer to a large, warmed serving dish, and garnish with grated lemon zest and stale bread cut into chunks.

1 lb. dried cannellini beans, soaked overnight

3 tbsp. olive oil

⅓ lb. pancetta, medium dice

⅓ lb. hot Italian sausage, outer casings removed, medium dice

1 onion, finely chopped

3 cloves garlic, minced

⅓ cup dry white wine

¼ cup parsley, chopped

Salt and pepper

Lemon zest

Stale bread, for serving

GREEN SOUP WITH GARLIC BREAD

Zuppa Verde   Serves 6

Preheat oven to 375°F.

Rub each slice of bread with a clove of garlic and toast in the oven for about 15 minutes, turning the slices for even browning.

Melt the butter in a large, deep saucepan over medium heat. Add the onion and sauté until tender and caramelized, about 10 minutes.

Add all the greens and cook over high heat until they are wilted, about 5 minutes, adding the baking soda to preserve color as you cook.

Add the potatoes and the stock, then cover and simmer over low heat until the greens are tender, about 15 minutes. Adjust for salt and pepper.

Place one slice of the garlic bread in each bowl and pour the soup over it to serve.

6 slices crusty bread

6 cloves garlic

1 tbsp. butter

1 large red onion, finely sliced

2 large bunches collard greens, mustard greens, or radish leaves, roughly chopped

2 cups baby spinach, roughly chopped

2 cups mâche, roughly chopped

1 tsp. baking soda

20 baby potatoes, sliced into ¼-inch rounds

3 cups vegetable stock (see recipe on page 264)

Salt and pepper

WHATEVER IS AVAILABLE VEGETABLE SOUP

Minestrone

Place all the *fondo* ingredients into a tall stockpot over medium heat and cook for about 10–15 minutes, until the vegetables are caramelized. Add the garlic and keep cooking on low for another 5 minutes. By now the beans should be wrinkled and the potatoes barely cooked. Add all the greens and cook until they have lost their moisture and are completely wilted.

Now add the tomato sauce, stirring to coat the vegetables completely. Add 4 cups of the stock, reduce by ⅓ over high heat, then add the pasta. If the soup looks too thick, add the rest of the stock.

When the pasta is cooked, pour the soup into bowls and top with grated Parmesan and extra-virgin olive oil.

TIP: Soup is a great place to use up spare pasta. Break up large noodles or just add small shapes whole.

For the *fondo*:

1 cup cannellini or borlotti
    beans, dried
1 cup potatoes, diced
Salt and pepper
¼ cup olive oil
1 cup onion, diced
½ cup red onion, diced
1 cup carrots, diced
1 cup celery, diced
½ cup fennel, diced
1 cup zucchini, diced

For the soup:

3 cloves garlic, finely
    chopped
1 bunch each: chard, kale
    or Tuscan cabbage,
    collard greens, spinach,
    stem ends removed, all
    roughly chopped
1 cup Fabio's Tomato
    Sauce (see recipe on
    page 18)
5 cups vegetable stock
    (see recipe on page 264)
1 cup any small pasta
Parmesan cheese, grated
Extra-virgin olive oil, for
    serving

DROWNED CLAMS

Vongole Affogate

Serves 4–6 as an appetizer

Put ⅓ of the clam juice or stock in a deep sauté pan with the clams, bring it to a boil, then put a lid on it and cook for about 5 minutes to let the clams steam open. Turn off the heat, remove the clams, and reserve the cooking liquid.

In a large pot, heat the olive oil and sauté the salami, carrots, onions, and celery until the onions and celery are translucent but not browned.

Add the reserved clam-cooking liquid, the remaining clam juice or stock, the potatoes, corn, and oregano, and season with salt and pepper. Simmer, uncovered, over medium heat for about 10 minutes or until the potatoes are tender.

Pull clams out of their shells and either chop them or leave them whole. Whisk the milk and flour in a bowl, then add it slowly to the broth, continuing to whisk until slightly thickened. Add the clams to the soup, then the parsley, and serve.

3 cups clam juice or fish stock (see recipe on page 261)

5 dozen Manila clams, in shells

2 tbsp. olive oil

2 slices spicy salami, chopped

2 carrots, finely diced

2 medium-size red onions, chopped

1 celery stalk, finely diced

15 baby potatoes, cut in quarters

1½ cups sweet corn, fresh if available, otherwise frozen

2 tbsp. fresh oregano

Salt and pepper

3 cups whole milk

2 tbsp. flour

2 tbsp. parsley, chopped

ARTICHOKE SOUP

Zuppa di Carciofi

Serves 4

Heat the oil in a Dutch oven over medium heat. Add the leeks, potatoes, artichokes or artichoke hearts, and garlic and cook for 25 minutes. Add the stock and/or water and the rosemary and bring to a boil over high heat.

Turn the heat down to medium and cook for 10–15 minutes, stirring often. Reduce to a simmer and cook until potatoes are softened.

Remove the soup from the heat and allow it to cool. Using a stick blender, puree. Adjust for salt and pepper and serve.

3 tbsp. vegetable oil

1 cup leeks, cleaned and chopped

2 small Yukon gold potatoes, scrubbed and diced

2 lb. baby artichokes, leaves removed, scrubbed, thinly sliced, and kept in lemon water; or good-quality canned artichoke hearts, drained

3 cloves garlic, minced

6 cups vegetable stock or water, or a combination of both

2 tbsp. chopped fresh rosemary

Salt and pepper

CRAZY WATER

Acquapazza

Serves 4

Depending on where you go in Italy, this is either a soup—if you add more leafy greens—or a base for a fish entrée where you cook the fish in it and then serve it as a side broth. If you don't have fish, as we didn't most of the time, serve this as a very basic vegetable soup.

In a large sauté pan over low heat, cook the crushed garlic in the oil until it is lightly caramelized. Add the wine, water, and salt and bring to a heavy boil.

Simmer for 5 minutes, add the baby spinach, let it wilt, then gently slip the fish fillets into the stock. Add the cherry tomatoes, basil, lemon or lime zest, and capers and continue simmering for another 5 minutes. Carefully turn the fish, and simmer for another 6 minutes, depending on the size of the fillets. The fish is done when the flesh falls apart easily when poked with a fork.

Remove the fish to 4 warm bowls. Bring the stock to a boil and spoon it over the fish. Serve topped with parsley and lemon wedges.

2 cloves garlic, crushed

2 tbsp. olive oil

2 cups dry white wine

2 cups water

1 tsp. salt

A handful of baby spinach

4 small fillets of snapper or salmon, 4–6 oz. each

30 cherry tomatoes, cut in half

1 cup basil leaves

Zest of 1 lemon or 1 lime

2 tbsp. capers, rinsed

2 tbsp. flat parsley leaves, torn

1 lemon, sliced into wedges

ITALIAN WEDDING SOUP

Zuppa del Matrimonio

Serves 6–8

This traditional southern Italian recipe celebrates the marriage of vegetables with meatballs in a heaven of soup. So it pretty much has nothing to do with a real wedding. Nobody who gets married in Italy eats this soup at the wedding. "Hey, let's get married! I can't wait to have meatballs!" Are you nuts?

Preheat the oven to 375°F.

Heat the olive oil in a large stockpot and cook the carrots, onion, and celery until soft and starting to caramelize, about 15 minutes.

While the vegetables sauté, make the meatballs. Mix the beef, eggs, breadcrumbs, Parmesan, salt, and pepper in a mixing bowl. Form into ½-inch balls and set on a baking sheet. Bake for 12–15 minutes.

Add the spinach to the sautéing vegetables and let it wilt. Then add the chicken stock to the vegetables and cook over high heat until it is somewhat reduced. Add the pasta to cook, and when the meatballs are ready, add them to the pot, too.

Boil 5 minutes and season with salt and pepper.

½ cup olive oil

1 cup carrots, diced

1 cup yellow onion, diced

1 cup celery, diced

1 lb. lean ground beef

2 eggs

⅓ cup panko breadcrumbs

3 tbsp. Parmesan cheese, grated

Salt and pepper

3 cups fresh baby spinach

3 quarts chicken stock (see recipe on page 260)

2 cups orzo pasta

TIP: Reducing stock increases flavor!

Ribollita   Serves 6–8

We always had a lot of leftovers, and this is kind of a green leaf soup that also uses stale bread. This is actually one of the few dishes that is better if you reheat it the next day, after you let the bread soak in and add extra stock. We call it soup but it's not soup. It's very thick, but as I said, in Italy unless it's pasta or rice we call it a soup.

Place the beans and their soaking liquid, plus about 2 more gallons of water, into a large pot over medium heat.

Meanwhile, in another large pot, caramelize the onion in the olive oil. When the onion is golden, slowly add the tomatoes and all the other vegetables and cook for 10 minutes or until they are softened. Now add all the cooking water left in the bean pot and half of the cooked beans.

Using a fork or a potato masher, smash the remaining beans, then add them to the soup.

Season with salt and pepper to taste and cook over low heat for 2 hours, covered with a lid.

Tear the bread slices into chunks and after the soup has cooked for 2 hours, add them to the pot and stir well. Simmer the soup for an additional 15 minutes, stirring as needed (it should be quite thick).

Turn off the heat and let the soup rest for half an hour with the lid on, then drizzle with extra-virgin olive oil.

1 lb. dried cannellini beans, soaked overnight in water

1 onion, sliced (plus 1 red onion, sliced—optional)

3 tbsp. olive oil

2 plum tomatoes, peeled and roughly chopped

1 bunch Swiss chard, roughly chopped

1 bunch black kale, roughly chopped

2 leeks, cleaned and roughly chopped

¼ head Savoy cabbage, roughly chopped

2 celery stalks, roughly chopped

Salt and pepper

8 1-inch-thick slices of stale homemade white bread toasted in the oven at 375°F for about 20 minutes (if you don't have homemade, any crusty white bread will do)

Extra-virgin olive oil, for drizzling

MY MOTHER'S TOMATO-BREAD SOUP

Pappa al Pomodoro

My grandpa used to eat this by using a wide piece of bread as a spoon—bread on bread! Go figure why he now has a nice round belly. Again, this is not really a soup.

Cut the bread into 1-inch chunks, place them on a sheet pan, and bake at 225°F for about 20 minutes or until dry. Remove the pan from the oven and raise the oven temperature to 325°F.

In a heavy saucepan, sauté the onion in the olive oil over medium heat for about 10 minutes, until the onion is caramelized, then add the garlic. When the garlic is almost browned, add the tomatoes and stir to coat with the oil and garlic. When the tomatoes start to turn mushy, add the tomato puree, some salt, and a generous grind of pepper. When the oil has turned the color of the tomatoes, add the bread and stir to combine.

Place the mixture in a Pyrex or other baking dish and bake for about 35–40 minutes. If it gets too dry, add a little stock or water.

Serve with hand-ripped basil leaves and extra-virgin olive oil on top.

1 loaf Tuscan or ciabatta bread

1½ cups olive oil

2 cups red onion, finely minced

10 medium-large garlic cloves, cut in large pieces

3 lb. really ripe fresh tomatoes or canned plum tomatoes, chopped

2 cups tomato puree

Salt and pepper

1½–2 cups water or vegetable stock, as needed

1 generous bunch basil

Extra-virgin olive oil, for serving

As you may have guessed by now, I was not a very well–behaved child. My mom loves to remind me of the time she tried to take me shoe shopping when I was a little kid and I knocked over two huge shelves of shoes the minute we got into the store. As she says now, "I kept telling myself that Fabio acted like this because he was intelligent. The truth was, we knew that he was just a naughty little thing." Every time I needed shoes after that, the store owners would close to the public and focus solely on us.

There's another little story she likes to tell about me. It took place on a very hot August afternoon. She always starts it with: "All of Fabio's friends were gone on vacation, but we were not." Then it goes on:

One afternoon, I had no idea what to do to make Fabio behave himself. I tried to play with him to help pass the time. He said that I didn't know how to play with his favorite toys. So I said, "Fabio, come with me to the supermarket and let's see if Daddy can come, too! We'll get an ice cream and I can do a bit of shopping."

He responded, "Okay, Mom, let's go." I should have known better.

We went to the store and I had Fabio by the hand. While we were in the store, I let go of Fabio's hand for a second and he disappeared. I turned around and he was gone. His dad and I split up, going in opposite directions to look for him. There weren't a lot of people, so it shouldn't have been difficult to find him, but it was. I was shouting his name when a voice over the loud-speaker said, "If any parents have lost their child, please come to the frozen food section."

There, the lady at the counter asked me, "What is your kid's name?" "Fabio," I said. She then said, "Well, here you are, ma'am. Would you like to explain to your child why you can't lay down on the bags of frozen vegetables?" We nodded, his father took him by the arm, and we walked away.

We asked him why he was lying on the vegetables and he responded, "I was really hot and it felt so nice to lay on the cold bags. Plus these berries are delicious and I'm hungry!"

Luckily, we didn't have to pay for the damaged bag because they understood he was only a child, but they did beg us not to bring Fabio back to the supermarket ever again.

Sorry, Mom! After that, pretty much every time I went out with someone I was kept on a dog leash, which my mom tied to one of the belt loops of my jeans. It had a little manual crank you could use to shorten and lengthen the leash, and she would let it out so I could run. But mostly she was forever having to reel me back in.

Things didn't get much better when I started school. On the first day, when I was six years old, I marched into the classroom and informed the teacher, "Look, I already know how to read and write, and I cook dinner for everybody, too." (I

was a big shot, even then.) It was true that my aunts and uncles had spent a lot of time teaching me, but the teacher just smiled and said I'd have to be patient with the other children while they learned. I wasn't patient at all, of course. I got bored and made trouble and all I wanted to do was go into the school kitchen with the cooks and help them prepare the meals for the students. My mom was constantly having to come in and meet with the teacher, and she would explain that it was exactly the same thing at home. They had no idea how to make me behave, either, and the only thing that kept me focused was cooking with my great-grandmother.

The one other creature that could make me calm down was my pet rabbit, Calimero, a little black bunny I named in honor of one of my favorite cartoon characters. I loved him so much, I took him everywhere with me. I even tucked him in bed with me at night. One day my mom came home and discovered Calimero had died suddenly. She didn't know how to tell me, so she decided to say that he had gone to a farm so he could find a girlfriend and have baby rabbits. After a little while, however, she realized that sooner or later Calimero would have to return home.

She began visiting pet stores, hoping to find a black rabbit to replace Calimero. She ended up finding one, but it had a white spot on the tip of its paw, and it was female. She bought it anyway, hoping that because I was only six, I wouldn't notice. She made up a story about the white spot on its paw, saying that while Calimero was at the farm, someone had cleaned his cage with bleach and he had stuck his paw into it. I continued to believe the story even after I discovered Calimero was a girl. Apparently I came in for dinner a few days after the new rabbit came home and told my family, "Do you know that we are all stupid? Calimero isn't a boy! He doesn't have any boy parts. He has girl parts! How silly we all are for not noticing!" Calimero 2.0, the girl rabbit, was my rabbit for years and years and lived happily ever after.

Even after Calimero died, I never forgot him. Or her. Many years later, one of the owners of the restaurant where I worked in Florence said, "Fabio, this evening I want you to cook me a rabbit."

I said, "Sure, just bring me the rabbit."

A couple of hours later, he returned with a live rabbit and told me to kill it and cook it. Thinking of Calimero, I replied that I would rather kill *him*. When he said, "If you don't cook this rabbit, I'll fire you," I said, "Go ahead. But I'm taking this rabbit with me." And with that, I took the rabbit and left without another word. Later he called and apologized and asked me to come back to work, and to this day I still don't eat rabbit.

> *On the first day [of school], when I was six years old, I marched into the classroom and informed the teacher, "Look, I already know how to read and write, and I cook dinner for everybody, too."*

PASTA, GNOCCHI, & RISOTTO

Affari Italiani

When I'm upset I don't want to be left alone. I want to be left alone in a bath of pasta.

There are three main kinds of pasta. There's "you're broke" pasta that you make when you have nothing but water and flour and salt, and it's good for shapes like orecchiette or small pasta you use for soup. If you add eggs to it, then you have regular pasta, which is a heavier, richer pasta. You can either eat it right away or let it dry to store it. We had a straw broom in our kitchen, and my mom would use it to sweep the floor and then put it between two chairs and hang fresh egg pasta over the stick to dry. The third kind of pasta is dry pasta from a box. It's made of semolina flour and most likely has no eggs. That's the best for making al dente pasta. You can have all kinds of pasta—lasagna, ravioli, gnocchi—but unless you have tried a true al dente plate of spaghetti, you can't say you've had pasta.

America, make your own pasta! It's simple! I make fresh pasta all the time. Sometimes I only have a half hour to cook and that's what I make because it's so easy.

Think about this: If you make your own pasta, you are in the 2 percent of the nation that knows how to do it. Don't you want to be in that 2 percent? If you don't have a quarter million dollar salary, making fresh pasta is another way to be in the 2 percent.

SPAGHETTI WITH GARLIC AND OLIVE OIL

Aglio e Olio

Serves 4

My mom used to cheat in this recipe, adding a small dollop of butter to help the sauce come together and not look oily.

Bring a large pot of salted water to a boil.

Heat the olive oil in a sauté pan over medium heat.

Start cooking the spaghetti in the water. While it cooks, sauté the garlic in the oil until it is very light brown, then add the red pepper flakes and turn the heat off or it will all burn.

When the pasta has cooked for one-third less time than the package directions suggest and is al dente, drain it and reserve some of the cooking water. Add the pasta, the butter, and about a third of a cup of cooking water to the garlic-red pepper mixture, cooking and shaking the pan over medium heat to create an emulsion with the water and the oil. Serve with the parsley on top and enjoy. You will need a bib!

½ cup olive oil

1 lb. dry spaghetti

5 cloves garlic, very thinly sliced

1 tbsp. red pepper flakes

1 tsp. butter

1 bunch parsley, chopped

TIP: The best way to overcook your pasta is to follow the package directions. Always cut the time by one-third.

DRUNKEN SPAGHETTI

Spaghetti Ubriachi

Serves 2

In Italy we feel bad throwing away even old wine, so we color our pasta water with it to get a little aroma of wine and a dramatic presentation. The flavor of the wine is in the water but you're not going to feel it, and you give leftover wine a last chance to be useful. The more wine you use, the redder the spaghetti will be—and this dish is all about the presentation, so you can use up to a whole bottle depending on how much you have around. You can also always buy an inexpensive bottle just for the recipe.

Bring the water and the wine to a boil in a large pot. Cook the pasta in it until the pasta is al dente (see tip on page 79). Drain, reserving a few tablespoons of the cooking liquid.

In a sauté pan large enough to hold the pasta, cook the pancetta in the butter until its fat has been rendered.

Add the spaghetti and about 1 tablespoon of the reserved cooking liquid to the sauté pan. Once the liquid has reduced, remove the pasta from the heat.

Add the ricotta and walnuts and mix with tongs. Top with the Pecorino and serve.

2 quarts water
1 bottle red wine (old or leftover is fine)
1 lb. dry spaghetti
½ lb. pancetta, diced
2 tbsp. butter
½ cup ricotta cheese
½ cup walnuts, chopped
Shaved Pecorino cheese to top

Call it four-cheese even if it's three-cheese or two-cheese. It doesn't matter. I mean, who's going to tell you, "Hey, no, you're cheating!"

Stop rolling and gently pull the skewer out, making sure you pull on the stick rather than the dough. Giving the stick a twist will help. You should end up with a long, thin, hollow noodle. Repeat with the rest of the dough and lay all your pici on a wire rack dusted with semolina flour to dry out slightly before using.

To make the ragu, place a saucepan large enough to hold all the sauce ingredients over medium heat. Add a splash of olive oil to the pan along with the onion and garlic and cook slowly for about 10 minutes, until the garlic is soft and lightly colored.

Add the bay leaves, rosemary, ground lamb, and tomatoes and season with salt and pepper. Stir well and bring to a boil. Turn the heat down, cover, and simmer gently for 2 hours. Check every 10–15 minutes, and if the sauce starts to look dry at any point, add some water.

Cook the pici noodles in salted boiling water for about 8–10 minutes, until cooked through but still al dente. Drain them and then stir them into the hot ragu sauce. Add a good splash of extra-virgin olive oil, then taste and season again if necessary. Serve with lots of freshly grated Parmesan.

PASTA HANDKERCHIEFS WITH CHICKEN

Pezze alla Gallina   Serves 4

Roll out the pasta to a thickness of less than 1/16 of an inch. If you use a machine, make it as thin as you can. Cut into 2 × 2-inch squares and let them rest on a cloth dusted with flour.

Preheat the oven to 400°F.

Heat 1 tablespoon of the oil in a heavy casserole over medium heat. Add the diced vegetables and garlic and sauté for 15 minutes, stirring every so often with a wooden spoon. Then add the pancetta and cook until the fat is completely released.

Take the chicken out of the wine, pat it dry, and reserve the wine. In a separate pan from the vegetables and pancetta, heat the rest of the oil, add the rosemary, and sear the chicken on all sides over medium heat. As the pieces are ready, take them out and place them in a roasting dish, then bake them in the oven for about 15 minutes. Once they're cooked, take them out and set them aside while you make the sauce.

Add the reserved wine to the pan with the diced vegetables, turn the heat to medium, and let it reduce almost completely. Then add the tomato paste, stir until it has completely dissolved, and add the broth and the parsley.

As the broth is reducing, pull the chicken meat off the bones and add it to the sauce. Keep reducing until all the liquid is gone.

Cook the pasta in salted boiling water. As soon as it floats, drain it and either combine all the pasta with the sauce, or serve the pasta with the sauce on top.

1 recipe Fresh Egg Pasta Dough (see recipe on page 12)

3 tbsp. olive oil

2 cups celery, finely diced

2 cups red onion, finely diced

2 cups carrots, finely diced

5 garlic cloves, crushed and roughly chopped

5 oz. pancetta, chopped

1 sprig rosemary

2 lb. chicken pieces, soaked overnight in 3 cups red wine

½ cup tomato paste

2 cups chicken stock, lukewarm (see recipe on page 260)

1 cup parsley leaves

Salt and pepper

BAKED ZITI

Ziti al Forno   Serves 4–6

Preheat the oven to the lowest broiler setting.

Bring a pot of salted water to a boil and cook the pasta for about 5–6 minutes.

Toss the pasta with the meat sauce, béchamel sauce, and Parmesan cheese, mixing until it is well coated.

Pour into an ungreased baking dish and cover with the mozzarella. Place the pan under the broiler and cook until the cheese is golden brown and bubbly.

Remove from oven and let rest before serving.

1 lb. dried ziti or penne pasta

2 cups Grandma's Meat Sauce (see recipe on page 23)

2 cups béchamel sauce (see recipe on page 268)

1 cup Parmesan cheese, grated

1 cup mozzarella cheese, shredded

NAKED RAVIOLI WITH FRESH TOMATO SAUCE

Gnudi al Pomodoro Fresco

Serves 4

Preheat the oven to 375°F.

Put the tomatoes in a deep sauté pan over medium heat and drizzle them with the olive oil. Season with salt and pepper and cook until you can easily smash them with a fork.

Layer some of the tomato sauce on the bottom of a baking dish and arrange the naked ravioli on top of it. Then put all the remaining sauce on the ravioli.

Bake for about 15–20 minutes, then drizzle the ravioli with the extra-virgin olive oil and top them with the basil leaves and Parmesan.

2 cups cherry tomatoes, cut in half

2 tbsp. olive oil

Salt and pepper

1 recipe Naked Ravioli (see recipe on page 29)

2 tbsp. extra-virgin olive oil

15–20 basil leaves

1 cup Parmesan cheese, grated

POTATO RAVIOLI

Ravioli di Patate

Serves 6–8

Serve these with any sauce in this book (not one from any other book—my ravioli are very sensitive).

Cut the potatoes into quarters and cook them in boiling water until soft, about 15–20 minutes. When they are slightly cooled, puree them using a potato ricer, or mash them with a fork. Combine the potatoes with the egg yolks, salt, pepper, nutmeg, and Parmesan cheese.

Heat the olive oil and butter in a sauté pan over medium heat and cook the onion, garlic, and sage for about 10 minutes until the vegetables are caramelized. Let them cool to room temperature, and add to the potato mixture.

Lay the sheets of pasta in front of you and place 1 tablespoon of filling every 2 inches just above the center of the sheet. Beat the egg with about a tablespoon of water in a small bowl. Then, using the tip of your finger, brush lightly around each lump of filling with the egg-and-water mixture. Fold the bottom half of the pasta sheet over the filled half.

Press down around the edges of the filling to remove any air bubbles and seal the filling in. Cut the pasta into individual ravioli with a zigzag cutter or knife. Repeat this procedure until you run out of filling.

Bring a large pot of water to a boil and add salt. Add the ravioli and cook until they rise to the top, about 3 minutes.

4–5 potatoes, russet or Idaho, peeled
2 egg yolks, plus 1 egg
Salt and pepper
A dash of nutmeg
½ cup Parmesan cheese, grated
¼ cup olive oil
4 tbsp. butter
1 medium onion, minced
3 cloves garlic, minced
1 sprig fresh sage, leaves only, finely minced
1 recipe Fresh Egg Pasta Dough, stretched into thin 4 x 8-inch sheets (see recipe on page 12)

TIP: You need much less filling per ravioli than you'd think. A spoonful is usually enough.

BUTTERNUT SQUASH RAVIOLI WITH BROWN BUTTER SAGE SAUCE

Ravioli di Zucca

Serves 6

In northern Italy, a traditionally wealthier area than Tuscany, they fill their pasta with meat, truffles, or expensive cheese. We had no money, so our pasta was filled with potato (as in the previous recipe) and squash. The squash are roasted, and the flavor that comes out is intense and sweet. Then you add the ricotta and the amaretto cookies. *What*? Amaretto cookies? This dish is sexiness at the purest level, with crispy sage on top. It is the dish for the person you're about to love, the person that you loved already and would like to love again, or for somebody who hates you, as it will make them love you.

Preheat the oven to 400°F.

Cut the squash in half lengthwise, remove the seeds, and roast face up on a baking sheet until soft when poked with a fork, about 45 minutes. Set aside to cool.

To make the filling, scoop out the cooled squash flesh and mix it in a bowl with the Parmesan, the ricotta, the amaretti, and salt and pepper to taste.

Lay the sheets of pasta in front of you and place 1 tablespoon of filling every 2 inches just above the center of the sheet.

Beat the egg with about a tablespoon of water in a small bowl. Then, using the tip of your finger, brush lightly around each lump of filling with the egg-and-water mixture. Fold the bottom half of the pasta sheet over the filled half.

Press down around the edges of the filling to remove any air bubbles and seal the filling in. Cut the pasta into individual ravioli with a zigzag cutter or knife. Repeat this procedure until you run out of filling.

Bring a large pot of water to a boil and add salt. Add the ravioli and cook until they rise to the top, about 3 minutes. Combine with the brown butter sage sauce and serve.

2 medium butternut squash

½ cup Parmesan cheese, finely grated

1 cup ricotta cheese

6 tbsp. ground amaretto cookies

Salt and pepper

1 recipe Fresh Egg Pasta Dough, rolled out in thin 4 x 8-inch sheets (see recipe on page 12)

1 egg

1 recipe Brown Butter Sage Sauce (see recipe on page 20)

TIP: Fresh ravioli cook faster than dried or refrigerated ravioli.

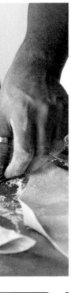

PESTO GNOCCHI

Gnocchi al Pesto

Serves 4

Bring a pot of salted water to a boil and start cooking the gnocchi.

While they are cooking, combine the pesto, stock, and cream in a saucepan over medium heat. Don't overheat it or the pesto will turn brown (still good to eat, but not good to look at anymore).

When the first gnocchi rise to the top of the pot, remove all the gnocchi with a slotted spoon and place them in the pan with the sauce. When they are all in, toss them once or twice to coat and turn the heat off immediately.

Transfer the gnocchi to a platter and top them with the basil leaves and pine nuts to serve.

1 recipe Potato-Ricotta Gnocchi (see recipe on page 14)

1 cup pesto sauce (see recipe on page 17)

¼ cup vegetable or chicken stock (see recipes on pages 264 and 260)

2 tbsp. heavy cream

20 basil leaves, preferably small

2 tbsp. pine nuts

TIP: Don't forget the notes on making and cooking gnocchi! (see page 14)

GNOCCHI WITH SAUSAGE AND LEEKS

Gnocchi con Salsiccia e Porri

Serves 4

Preheat the oven to 375°F.

Clean the leeks well and slice the white and pale green portions into thin rounds.

Put the butter in a deep sauté pan over medium heat and add the garlic and sausage. Using a wooden spoon, crumble the sausage as it cooks. When it is completely cooked, it will turn from a reddish to a brown-gray color. You can also use whole sausages (as pictured), in which case brown them on all sides.

Add the wine to the pan and start to reduce it. While it is reducing, toss the leeks with the olive oil, salt, and pepper and spread them on a baking sheet. Roast in the oven for 15 minutes.

Once the wine has reduced and the leeks are roasted, drop the gnocchi in a pot of salted boiling water. As soon as the first gnocchi rise to the top of the pot, remove all the gnocchi and add them to the pan with the sausage mixture. Mix the gnocchi well with the sauce, add the leeks, and mix them in.

To serve, drizzle with extra-virgin olive oil.

2 leeks

1 tbsp. butter

2 tbsp. garlic, minced

1 lb. ground sausage meat or 1 lb. whole Italian sausages

1 cup dry white wine

2 tbsp. olive oil

Salt and pepper

1 recipe Potato-Ricotta Gnocchi (see recipe on page 14)

Extra-virgin olive oil, for drizzling

GNOCCHI WITH MEAT SAUCE AND RICOTTA SALATA

Gnocchi al Ragu

Serves 4

Ricotta salata is an aged ricotta that has been washed with salt water. It's also great in sandwiches and with fruit or dried fruit.

Preheat the oven to 425°F.

Heat the meat sauce and set it aside.

Cook the gnocchi according to the package directions. Wait . . . there is no package! Of course not! You are making your own gnocchi and kicking ass with this book!

Okay then, cook the gnocchi in salted boiling water. Take them all out with a slotted spoon as soon as the first ones rise to the top, and toss them with the meat sauce. Once the gnocchi are in the sauce, put everything in a baking dish. Top with the ricotta salata and bake for about 10 minutes or until the ricotta is bubbling.

2 cups Grandma's Meat Sauce (see recipe on page 23)

1 recipe Fabio's Potato-Ricotta Gnocchi, with 1 additional cup of flour added to the dough to make the gnocchi a little bit harder (see recipe on page 14)

About 1½ cups ricotta salata, shaved in wide ribbons

RICOTTA GNOCCHI WITH SQUASH BLOSSOMS AND CLAMS

Ricotta Gnocchi con Vongole e Fiori di Zucca

Serves 4

Put the olive oil in a large, deep sauté pan over medium heat. Add the squash blossoms, saffron, and clams and cover with a lid. Once the clams start to open (about 2 minutes), add the wine and the butter.

Start cooking the gnocchi in salted boiling water. While they're cooking, add a pinch of salt, some pepper, and the basil to the pan with the clams (by now they should all have opened; discard any that have not).

When the first gnocchi rise to the top of the pot, remove all the gnocchi and put them directly into the pan with the sauce, stirring to coat them, and cook for another 3 minutes. Serve immediately.

2 tbsp. olive oil

10–12 squash blossoms, sliced in thirds

A pinch of saffron

20 clams, in shell

1 cup white wine

2 tbsp. butter

1 recipe Potato-Ricotta Gnocchi (see recipe on page 14)

Salt and pepper

20 basil leaves, roughly chopped

MUSHROOM RISOTTO

Risotto ai Funghi

Serves 4

We didn't make this often, because mushroom season in Italy—in late summer or early autumn—is short. We loved pancetta, which adds a great richness and saltiness, but we didn't always have it, so my mom would never really mention it. She just called it mushroom risotto and put it on the table. My dad would say, "There is no pancetta!" and she'd just say, "No." Or he'd say, "There is pancetta!" and she'd say, "Yes!" She was in total denial about how she had made it the previous time, and we didn't dare to call her on it.

Heat 3 tablespoons of the butter in a large heavy-bottomed sauté pan over medium heat. Add the pancetta and cook until golden brown, then add the onion and mushrooms with a pinch of salt and sauté until they soften, about 10 minutes.

Add the rice and cook with the rest of the ingredients for a few minutes. Pour in the red wine and simmer until absorbed almost completely.

Start adding the stock one ladle at a time, just enough to cover the rice. As the stock is absorbed and the rice cooks, stir in more stock, each time adding just enough to cover the rice. Stir often, making sure it doesn't stick to the bottom of the pan.

Once you have added all the stock and the rice is tender, remove from heat and stir in the remaining butter and the Parmesan. Adjust for salt and pepper and serve with the rest of the bottle of wine on the side.

4 tbsp. butter

4 slices pancetta, diced

1 yellow onion, diced

1 lb. oyster or shiitake mushrooms, sliced

Salt and pepper

1⅓ cups Arborio rice

1 cup red wine

2 quarts beef or chicken stock, hot (see recipes on pages 263 and 260)

⅓ cup Parmesan cheese, grated, plus more to taste

SAFFRON RISOTTO

Risotto Milanese   Serves 6

This risotto isn't really considered an entrée, but a side dish for Osso Bucco (see recipe on page 135). Because of this, it requires a different cooking method than other risottos—instead of stirring, you let it sit and stir it either very little or not at all. This creates a creamier risotto which holds the Osso Bucco sauce well.

In a medium saucepan, cook the onion and the pancetta in the butter over medium heat until the onion is tender but not brown. Stir in the stock, saffron, rice, salt, and pepper. Bring to a rolling boil, then reduce the heat to low. Cover with a tight-fitting lid.

Continue cooking for 15 minutes without lifting the lid. Remove from heat. Let stand, covered, for 5–8 minutes. The rice should be tender but still slightly firm, and the mixture should be creamy. If necessary, stir in a little water to reach desired consistency.

Serve immediately.

2 tbsp. butter
¼ cup onion, finely chopped
1 cup pancetta, diced
3 cups chicken or beef stock (see recipes on pages 260 and 263)
1 tsp. saffron
1 cup Arborio rice
½ tsp. salt
A dash of pepper

SEAFOOD RISOTTO

Risotto di Mare

Serves 4

Drain the tomatoes and—if using canned clams—the clams, reserve all liquid, and set the clams aside. Combine the tomato juice and clam juice (if you have it) in a large measuring cup, then add enough stock to make 3 cups of liquid.

Pour the olive oil into a medium saucepan and cook the clams and mussels over medium heat until all the shells have opened (for a faster result, cover with a lid). Discard any clams or mussels that have not opened, then add the calamari and remove from heat.

Put the butter in a large sauté pan and cook the onions and garlic over medium heat until onions are tender but not brown. Add the rice, wine, salt, thyme, and red pepper flakes and reduce, stirring often, until the wine has disappeared.

Start adding the stock one ladle at a time, just enough to cover the rice. As the stock is absorbed and the rice cooks, stir in more stock, each time adding just enough to cover the rice. Stir often, making sure it doesn't stick to the bottom of the pan.

Once you have added all the stock and the rice is tender, remove from heat and stir in all the seafood. Cover and let stand for 2 minutes.

Stir in the parsley and serve immediately.

½ cup canned crushed tomatoes

10 clams or one 7½-oz. can minced clams

2 cups fish or shellfish stock (see recipes on pages 261 and 262)

2 tbsp. olive oil

8 mussels

½ cup calamari, bodies and tentacles, sliced

1 tbsp. butter

½ cup onion, chopped

2 cloves garlic, minced

2 cups Arborio rice

⅓ cup dry white wine

1 tsp. salt

1 tsp. fresh thyme, chopped

A dash of red pepper flakes

2 tbsp. parsley, chopped

RISOTTO WITH PUMPKIN AND WALNUTS

Risotto alle Noci e Zucca
Serves 4

Place 3 tablespoons of the butter in a large heavy-bottomed sauté pan over medium heat. Add the onions and a pinch of salt and a few grinds of pepper and sauté until the onions start to soften, about 5 minutes.

Add the rice and cook for a few minutes until it is transluscent, then add the wine and simmer until almost completely absorbed.

Start adding the stock one ladle at a time, just enough to cover the rice, stirring continuously. As the stock is absorbed and the rice cooks, stir in more stock, just enough each time to cover the rice. Once you have added all the stock and the rice is tender, remove it from the heat and stir in 1 tablespoon of butter.

In a large skillet, melt the last tablespoon of butter and sear the pumpkin until golden brown on all sides. Transfer it to a plate and deglaze the pan with the pear juice, scraping all the brown bits from the bottom. (See page 21 for a tip on deglazing.) Reduce by half and set aside.

Gently fold the seared pumpkin into the risotto, reserving a few pieces for garnish. Serve the risotto warm, drizzled with the pear sauce and sprinkled with the reserved pumpkin and a few candied or regular walnuts..

5 tbsp. butter

1 small onion, diced

Salt and pepper

2 cups Arborio rice

1 cup red wine

2 quarts vegetable stock, hot (see recipe on page 264)

2 cups pumpkin, skin and seeds removed, diced into ¼-inch pieces

⅓ cup pear juice

½ cup candied or regular walnuts (see note below for candied walnuts recipe)

NOTE: To make candied walnuts, combine 2 cups of sugar with 3 cups of water in a pot and heat over low heat, stirring until the sugar is dissolved. Bring it to a boil, and the moment it boils, add 2–3 cups of walnuts, turn down the heat, and simmer them for at least an hour (2 hours is better—the longer you simmer them, the more sugar they absorb). The syrup should remain golden brown throughout. If you see it is turning a darker brown, add a bit of water. Remove the nuts from the liquid with a slotted spoon. Heat 2–3 cups of extra light olive oil to 350°F in a deep sauté pan, just enough to barely cover all the walnuts, and fry the walnuts until they are golden. Remove the nuts from the oil to drain on paper towels. I always do more than I need so I can have some around. Also, you can save the oil and use it again for frying.

TIP: If you don't have a thermometer to check your oil, get a wooden spoon and stick the flat part into the oil. Wood retains moisture inside, and oil and water don't do well together, so when your oil is hot enough for frying, bubbles will appear around the spoon. If they are tiny, your oil is still too cold. When you see real bubbles, it's ready for frying.

NOT-SO-BLACK SQUID INK RISOTTO

Nero di Seppia

Serves 4

Bring the stock to a boil and keep it warm.

In a large saucepan, heat the olive oil and butter over medium heat. Add the shallots and cook until well caramelized.

Add the rice and stir until it's translucent. Pour in the wine and reduce until all the liquid is gone, then add the ink and enough stock to just cover the rice. Stir continuously until the rice absorbs the liquid. Repeat, adding a ladle of stock at a time and allowing it to be absorbed, until all the stock is used. Before the last ladle goes in, add the squid to the pan.

When the risotto is cooked, add the cream. Stir and season with salt and pepper. Serve with the chopped parsley on top.

6 cups fish stock (see recipe on page 261)

3 tbsp. olive oil

3 tbsp. butter

2 shallots, finely chopped

2 cups Arborio rice

¼ cup white wine

2 tsp. of squid ink (ask at your fish market to buy this ink obtained from living squid—I doubt that the calamari you buy will still be alive!)

10 whole squid, cleaned and sliced into rings (about 2 cups)

1 tbsp. heavy cream

Salt and pepper

¼ cup parsley, chopped

RISOTTO WITH SHRIMP AND PANCETTA

Risotto ai Gamberi   Serves 4

In a large saucepan, cook the pancetta and a bit of pepper in the olive oil over medium heat until the pancetta fat has rendered and the pancetta is crisp and golden brown. Remove 3 large tablespoons of pancetta and reserve for garnish.

Add the rice to the pan and toss with the pancetta and oil so that it absorbs the fat.

Add enough chicken stock to cover the rice and bring it to a simmer. Now add the shrimp and bring the liquid quickly back to a boil. Once it has boiled, bring it down to a simmer and stir until all the stock is absorbed.

Continue adding the stock one ladle at a time, just enough to cover the rice. As the stock is absorbed and the rice cooks, stir in more stock, adding just enough each time to cover the rice. Stir often, making sure it doesn't stick to the bottom of the pan.

Taste the rice to see if it is cooked (if it isn't, add more stock—or water if you're out of stock), then mix in the butter and Parmesan cheese.

To serve, garnish with reserved pancetta, chopped parsley, and lemon zest.

2 tbsp. olive oil

½ lb. pancetta, diced

Pepper

2 cups Arborio rice

2 quarts chicken stock (see recipe on page 260)

2 cups small shrimp, heads off and deveined, tails on (frozen is fine)

1 tbsp. butter

1 cup Parmesan cheese, grated

2 tbsp. parsley, chopped

Zest of 1 lemon

One of our family traditions was that after the first early-autumn rain, my grandpa and I would go out hunting for mushrooms. When the rain came, I knew I would be getting up at four in the morning and going with him to look for big porcini mushrooms. We would keep some and sell some. We could easily make a couple of hundred dollars with about ten pounds of mushrooms, and my grandpa was so good at finding them that he could fill the trunk of his car.

Once, when I was about eleven years old, we were heading out on a mushroom expedition in the car at around five in the morning and a deer dashed across the road. We hit him in the head by accident, the car went into a ditch, and the deer was dead. It was frightening, but we were okay and Grandpa cheered, "This is meat for two months!" This was like winning the venison lottery!

So my grandpa slit the deer's throat with his mushroom knife, let it bleed, and then we loaded the animal into the car. We opened the trunk, folded the backseat down, and put the corpse in the back, with the two hind legs hanging out. When we got home, it was two in the afternoon, so my great-grandma was there but my mom, dad, and grandma were at work. Grandpa put the deer on the kitchen table, looked at it, and said, "We should take it to the butcher."

Now, about a year before this, I had mastered the skill of butchering meat properly at the butcher shop where my grandma cleaned. For Easter, the butcher had given us a whole lamb. My grandpa didn't know what to do with it, so we brought it back to the butcher and he took it apart. I thought it was fascinating, and I told him I wanted to learn how to do it. People don't like to think about where meat comes from, but if you've ever eaten meat, someone had to slaughter, skin, and butcher the animal first.

The butcher said, "Come here after school and I'll teach you how to butcher." My real reward for going there was knowledge, but I also got a piece of meat every night—a nice steak or a lamb shank or a head or something. I figured every time I went there, I worked three or four hours and I got food for my family, so I did it five days a week.

When we hit the deer and my grandpa said we should take it to the butcher, I announced, "I got this! I know how to do it!" Now, what I was used to butchering was a carcass—no skin, no guts, the whole animal already slaughtered, sectioned in half, and cleaned. So I said, "We've got to cut it open and then in half," like I knew what I was talking about. We turned the deer legs up on the table and cracked him open like I'd seen the butcher do. Inside, there were about *ninety pounds* of guts. Think about my kitchen table. There was a deer on top of it. My great-grandma, in her wheelchair, was holding the legs like she was overseeing a birth.

I started to cut open the deer—the ribs, everything—with a giant knife. Only then did I think to say, "Let's get a bucket to collect the guts." All we had was a mop bucket. My grandpa held it while I tipped the deer down. Maybe fifteen percent of the guts went into the bucket and the rest went all over the kitchen floor. It was completely covered in two inches of blood, guts, and worse (if I told you what the worse was, you'd lose your appetite!). Then the mess ran slowly onto the balcony, into the hallway, and underneath the furniture. My grandpa was moaning, "How are we going to . . . ?" He couldn't even finish his sentence.

My great-grandma was in her wheelchair and couldn't move because of the mess. It was a horrible scene. It looked like a bomb had gone off at the zoo. I kept shouting, "I got this! We'll clean up! Listen!" And since I was the only one with a plan, even though I was just eleven years old, everyone *did* listen.

We left the guts on the floor until I was able to use the knife to get the deer's legs and head off. Then we decided to wrap everything in the tablecloth and tie it up in a package with butcher's twine. Basically, it was a gigantic sack of blood. I was *covered* in guts. My grandpa's shoes were soaking wet with blood and guts. You have no idea how much stuff is packed inside a deer. And there we were, in a second-floor apartment in Florence—this was not a butcher shop, where you could hose everything off a stainless-steel table and out the door to the street.

By now it was seven-thirty at night. We flushed whatever we could down the toilet. We put the solid parts in the trashcan. And let's not talk about the smell. Let's not talk about the fact that the deer was still on the kitchen table

wrapped in the tablecloth. Let's not talk about the fact that my mom, my dad, and my grandma were coming home from work in twenty minutes. Let's keep focused on the fact that everything was still on the floor, because two hours or twenty would not have been enough to clean up this disaster. We didn't have enough towels or enough brooms. We were in no way equipped to cover the murder scene. My mom walked into the apartment, screamed, "What happened here?" and threw up. After she recovered, she asked every person in the building for pieces of fabric, old newspaper, anything they had, and we put everything on the floor to absorb the mess.

At two in the morning, the deer was still on the table and its skin was still on. So my grandpa called the butcher and said, "You need to come over here with your truck and get this thing out of my house." The butcher came and they tried to take the carcass down the narrow stairs, but they got stuck. Finally, they tossed the deer out the window and put it in the truck. I spent the whole night with the butcher, cleaning it. We got 150 pounds of meat and boiled the bones for stock. We didn't waste an ounce. Everyone was happy. It was a nightmare, but we had meat for six months, which was about how long it took for the smell to get out of the furniture. The take-home from this story is (parents, are you listening?): Never trust your child when he says he can butcher a deer on your kitchen table.

MEAT

La Carne

I love meat. I was a meat-and-potatoes guy when I was four, but we had no meat so I was just a potatoes guy.

In Italy, one of your best friends is your butcher. From the south to the north of the country, we have a lot of game, birds, pork, and other meats, but when you shop, you don't buy meat because you feel like lamb or pork or beef. You go to the butcher and ask, "What do you have today?" And he gives you the best of what they have for a price you can afford. It's the same thing most of the time when you go to a restaurant. They don't give you a menu. And if they do give you a menu, they tell you not to look at it because they want to suggest something.

When I would go food shopping with my grandma, she would call the butcher and say, "We're coming!" and we'd go there and pick up a little brown paper package in a plastic bag. She'd say, "How much do I owe you?" without even looking at it, and he'd give the price. We would walk the mile and a half home, and all the way I'd ask what was inside. My grandma would always say we had to wait until we got home, so we'd spend the walk guessing: Lamb? Pork? We almost never bought veal, because it was expensive, but sometimes the butcher would give it to my grandma in exchange for work. Any of the veal recipes here can just as easily be made with beef or even chicken in some cases. In Italy, meat is never the center of a meal, since there are so many other dishes being served as well. Whether you can afford only certain kinds of meat and not very much of them, like my family, or whether you can have whatever you like whenever you like, it's just one part of the dining experience. When you're eating a whole bunch of antipasto and a plate of pasta before your meat course, it doesn't have to be big or expensive to satisfy.

Still, I love meat. I was a meat-and-potatoes guy when I was four, but we had no meat so I was just a potatoes guy. Now that I can afford it, I love to buy a good, fatty steak. I also love pork, and one of my favorite dishes is the Nighttime Pork on page 117.

SAUSAGE AND BEANS STEWED IN TOMATO

Salsiccia e Fagioli ll'Uccelletto

Serves 4

Heat the olive oil in a heavy-bottomed pan over medium heat and add the garlic, red pepper flakes, and sausage. Cook until the sausage is browned.

Add the chicken stock and the tomatoes and simmer for 15 minutes. Add the beans and the sage and keep cooking over medium heat until the beans are cooked, about 45 minutes to 1 hour. If the mixture becomes dry, add a little water.

Serve with the Parmesan and parsley on top.

3 tbsp. olive oil

5 cloves garlic, chopped

1 tsp. red pepper flakes

4 sweet Italian sausages, cut in half

3 cups chicken stock (see recipe on page 260)

1 cup canned tomatoes, crushed

1 cup dried cannellini beans

1 sprig sage

½ cup Parmesan cheese, grated

2 tbsp. parsley, chopped

Porco di Notte

Serves 8

In Italy, what we call pork butt is literally the upper part of the leg attached to the pig's ass. In America, it means the front shoulder of the pig. Either way, it's cheap. All you have to do is let it cook super slow in the oven. You can change the rub, but otherwise there's nothing else to do but put it in the oven and forget about it.

Preheat the oven to 250°F.

Using a mortar and pestle, smash the fennel/rosemary/sage mixture with the salt and some pepper. Rub the pork with the dry spice mix.

Put the carrots, onions, fennel, garlic, and thyme into a large roasting pan. Add the stock and the wine, then rest the pork on top of the vegetables. Cover any vegetables not under the pork with aluminum foil, and put the pan in the oven.

Cook for 10–12 hours. The pork is done when you can pull it apart with a fork. Discard vegetables.

Serve on a gigantic cutting board with a big knife and a fork, so everyone can take as much as they want.

2 tbsp. fennel seeds,
  2 tbsp. dried rosemary,
  2 tbsp. dried sage, all
  mixed together
1 tbsp. sea salt
Pepper
12 lb. pork butt or shoulder,
  on the bone
4 carrots, roughly chopped
3 onions, roughly chopped
2 fennel bulbs, roughly
  chopped
1 head garlic, cloves
  peeled and smashed
2 bunches fresh thyme
2 cups chicken stock (see
  recipe on page 260)
3 cups dry white wine

BORED LAMB IN CHIANTI

Stufato al Chianti

Serves 6

Make sure that your lamb is really bored on the stove, because unless it sits there forever it's not going to be tender.

In a large Dutch oven, combine the oil, garlic, bay leaves, and rosemary over medium heat. Cook for 5 minutes, then add the onions, carrots, and celery. Turn the heat up to medium high and cook for about 15 minutes to *really* caramelize them.

Add the lamb and stir continuously until the meat has lost its red color on all sides. Remove the rosemary and bay leaves and season with salt and pepper. Stir, then add the wine and let it reduce for 20 minutes over medium heat.

Add ½ cup of the broth and the butter, cover the Dutch oven, and cook until the meat is soft, adding more broth as needed, about 20–45 minutes depending on the amount of fat in the meat. Taste the juices in the pot, adjust for salt and pepper, mix very well, and reduce, still over medium heat, for 10 minutes. Turn off the heat, remove the meat from the sauce, and set aside.

While the meat is resting, whisk the egg yolks and lemon juice in a bowl. Continuing to whisk at a fast pace, pour the mixture into the juices in the Dutch oven. When all the yolk mixture is incorporated into the sauce, put the Dutch oven back on low heat and, if too thick, add the remaining broth.

Place the meat back into the pot, bring it to a boil, and serve hot with fresh parsley on top.

½ cup olive oil

10 cloves garlic

8 bay leaves

1 sprig rosemary

2 cups red onion, chopped

1 cup carrots, chopped

2 cups celery, chopped

2 lb. boned lamb shoulder, cubed into 1½-inch pieces

Salt and pepper

2 cups Chianti wine

1 cup beef stock (see recipe on page 263)

2 tbsp. butter

4 egg yolks

1 tbsp. lemon juice

1 cup parsley, chopped

TIP: The leaner the lamb, the longer it takes to cook. For best flavor, ask your butcher for slightly fattier lamb.

MY GRANDMA'S OVERCOOKED VEAL SHANKS

Stracotto Della Nonna

Serves 6

This is not really overcooked. My grandpa was always so eager to eat it that he would always tell Grandma, "You're going to overcook it! Did you taste it? Is it ready? Take it out!" And Grandma would say, "No! It's not ready! I know you're just hungry!" My house was a circus. We would bet 10,000 lire, and the winner was whoever guessed the moment when Grandpa would start to bother everyone about the shank being ready.

This recipe is not for a whole leg of veal because no one wants to buy that, but I like the dramatic presentation of the veal with the bone in it shown in the picture. With boneless meat it's easier to cook and will taste almost the same.

Preheat the oven to 325°F.

Place the meat in a colander with the flour, salt, and pepper and toss until the veal is well coated (the excess flour will fall away through the colander holes).

Heat the olive oil in a Dutch oven and sauté the garlic and rosemary for about 10 minutes over low heat. Add the meat and brown it on all sides. (If it releases some water, that's okay. Don't freak out, you won't need to learn how to swim!)

Add the wine to the Dutch oven and let it reduce slightly, for 15 minutes. Adjust for salt and pepper, add the tomatoes, cover, and bake for 2½ hours, adding stock as needed to keep the pan from drying out. The meat should be soft and very juicy.

Use a slotted spoon to transfer the meat to a large serving platter. Reduce the remaining sauce in the casserole over medium heat and serve with the lamb.

3 lb. veal shoulder or shank cut into 2-inch pieces, preferably boneless
2 tbsp. unbleached flour
Salt and pepper
½ cup olive oil
10 cloves garlic, crushed
2 sprigs rosemary
2 cups red wine
2 lb. canned tomatoes, drained, mixed with 1 tbsp. tomato paste
1 cup beef stock (see recipe on page 263)

ITALIAN STUFFED BEEF

Braciole

The Italian way to stretch a dollar is to pound your beef very thin, fill it with something, and roll it. We call anything rolled this way an *involtino*.

Heat the tomato sauce in a small saucepan.

Meanwhile, place the beef in batches of 2 pieces between sheets of plastic wrap and pound them to about ⅓ of an inch thick with the pitted side of a meat mallet.

Lay a slice of prosciutto on each piece of flattened beef, and top each one with about 1 tablespoon of olive oil, minced garlic, and Parmesan. Roll the pieces up like cigars. Using a skewer, pierce a hole in the center of each roll, and insert a sprig of rosemary to secure it.

Heat the remaining oil in a large sauté pan with a lid. Sear the beef rolls on all sides, seasoning with salt and pepper as you sear.

Cover the rolls with tomato sauce and cook, covered, over medium heat for approximately 10 minutes, or until they are cooked through.

3 cups Fabio's Tomato Sauce (see recipe on page 18)

8 pieces beef shoulder or blade, 3 oz. each, cut to about ⅓-inch thick

8 slices prosciutto, or ham if you prefer

9 tbsp. olive oil

3 tbsp. garlic, minced

⅔ cup Parmesan cheese, grated

8 sprigs rosemary (pick ones with a firm stalk)

Salt and pepper

BRAISED GOAT WITH FENNEL AND RED ONION

Capra al Finocchio

Goats in Italy are the only animals that you can both name and eat. A lot of people keep them as backyard pets and treat them like domestic animals. They eat anything, so they're easy to keep, and they're very strong. They also give a lot of milk and are much cheaper to maintain than cows. Goats are common animals in Italy, but it's only common to eat them in certain regions, like Tuscany, Umbria, and Emilia-Romagna.

Combine the marinade ingredients. Season the goat meat with salt and pepper and place with the marinade in a sealed plastic bag or bags. Refrigerate overnight.

Preheat the oven to 400°F.

Remove the goat from marinade and pat dry. Strain the marinade and reserve the liquid only.

Heat the butter until it starts to sizzle over medium-high heat in a deep sauté pan large enough to hold the goat meat.

Add the meat and brown slowly over medium-low heat, turning frequently for about 15 minutes until golden brown on all sides.

Remove the meat and set aside, then remove all the fat in the pan except 2–3 tablespoons. Put the onions and garlic into the pan and sauté over medium heat until the onions are soft and translucent, adding a bit of butter if you like.

Pour the reserved marinade into the pan, bring to a boil, and reduce by half (about 15 minutes on high heat). Put the meat back into the pan and add the fennel seeds and enough stock to almost cover the meat.

Turn heat to high, bring to a boil, then reduce to a low simmer. Cover and place in the oven for about 3 hours, turning occasionally until the meat is tender and falls apart at the touch of a fork.

For the marinade:

1 cup red wine

½ cup olive oil

10 cloves garlic, crushed

2 large sprigs rosemary, leaves only

1 sprig thyme, leaves only

1 bay leaf

1 tbsp. fennel seed

For the meat:

3 lb. goat meat, shoulder or legs, cut into cubes about 3–4 inches

Salt and pepper

3 tbsp. butter, plus a dollop more—optional

1½ large onions, diced

2 cloves garlic, crushed

1 tbsp. fennel seed

2½ cups beef stock (see recipe on page 263)

FRIED VEAL CUTLETS

Milanese di Vitello

This is great for a family-style dinner. Squeeze a bunch of Roasted Lemons (see recipe on page 25) on it and serve it on a wooden cutting board. Kids will love it.

Place the meat between 2 sheets of plastic wrap and pound it with the pitted side of a meat mallet until it is about ½-inch thick. Season each cutlet generously on both sides with salt and pepper.

Place the flour in a low open container. Beat the eggs with the water and put them in a similar open container. Then mix the breadcrumbs and the Parmesan and place them in a third container.

Coat both sides of each cutlet in flour, then egg, and finally breadcrumbs. (While dredging in the crumbs, feel free to press a bit with the palm of your hand in order to make the crumbs stick better to the meat.) Set aside.

Heat the olive oil in a sauté pan over medium-high heat and cook each cutlet for 2–3 minutes per side or until the outside is golden brown.

As the cutlets are cooked, place them on a paper towel to absorb the oil.

Season again if necessary and serve with lemon slices.

6 veal cutlets, 4 oz. each (skinless, boneless chicken breasts can also be used)

Salt and pepper

1½ cups flour

3 large eggs, beaten

2 tbsp. water

2 cups panko breadcrumbs (or regular breadcrumbs)

½ cup Parmesan cheese, grated

6 tbsp. olive oil

1 lemon, cut into 6 wedges, for garnish

Polpettone della Nonna

Even with the oven on low, the outside of meat loaf dries out. My grandma used to spread tomato paste on the meat halfway through baking to keep it moist. Try it; the meat will stay juicy and delicious while the inside finishes cooking.

Preheat the oven to 350°F.

Heat the olive oil in a cast-iron pan and sear the garlic cloves until golden on both sides, then transfer them to a plate and mash them.

Add the onion to the pan with a pinch of salt and sauté until translucent. Stir in the carrot and celery and cook together until softened. Remove from heat.

In a large mixing bowl, combine the ground chuck with the eggs, sautéed vegetables, roasted garlic, tomato sauce, parsley, and cheeses. Season with salt and pepper and combine everything, making sure not to overwork the meat.

Transfer the mixture to a baking sheet and shape it into a loaf. Bake the meat loaf uncovered for 1 hour or until the internal temperature reaches 160°F. If using the optional tomato paste to coat the outside of the meat loaf, like Fabio's grandma, remove the pan after 30 minutes, spread the paste over the top of the meat loaf, and place it back in the oven for another 30 minutes to finish cooking.

Meanwhile, make the sauce by combining the tomato sauce, beef stock, and brown sugar in a small pot and bringing to a simmer. Cook for about 15 minutes until reduced to a thick consistency. Whisk in the dark chocolate until melted, then add the cream. Stir to combine, and serve on the side with the meat loaf.

For the meat loaf:

2 tbsp. olive oil

10 cloves garlic

1 small yellow onion, diced

Salt and pepper

1 large carrot, diced

2 celery stalks, diced

2 lb. ground chuck

4 eggs

½ cup Fabio's Tomato Sauce (see recipe on page 18)

⅓ cup parsley, minced

1 cup ricotta cheese

½ cup Parmesan cheese, grated

⅔ cup tomato paste (optional)

For the sauce:

1 cup Fabio's Tomato Sauce (see recipe on page 18)

½ cup beef stock (see recipe on page 263)

1 tbsp. brown sugar

2 tbsp. dark chocolate, chopped

2 tbsp. heavy cream

FABIO'S MOM'S MEATBALLS

Polpettine

This is probably the best meatball you ever had in your life, or perhaps second only to the one your grandma makes. It's certainly easier, because there is no bothering Grandma here. The best thing about these meatballs is that they stay super moist regardless of how much you cook or overcook them. The tomato sauce preserves the moisture. Everything about meatballs calls for soft and moist. Everything about cooking something in the oven calls for hot and dry. Soft and moist does not go with hot and dry, so meatballs should cooked on the stovetop in marinara sauce.

Place all ingredients except the tomato sauce, the parsley, and the extra-virgin olive oil in a medium-size bowl and mix thoroughly by hand until they are completely combined and the mixture is uniformly firm.

Coat your hands in olive oil, and form balls slightly bigger than a golf ball.

Heat the tomato sauce in a saucepan over medium heat, then drop the meatballs into the sauce and add enough water to allow the sauce to reduce and simmer but not so much that the sauce is totally liquid. Cook for about 10 minutes on one side, then turn the meatballs over, add some more water, and cook for another 10 minutes, using a spoon to cover the meatballs with the sauce as they simmer. Remove from heat and let rest for 5 minutes.

Serve with chopped parsley, salt and pepper, more Parmigiano-Reggiano, and a drizzle of extra-virgin olive oil, of course!

1 lb. ground beef

4 oz. whole milk ricotta cheese

1 cup Parmigiano-Reggiano cheese, grated

1 cup panko breadcrumbs

1 egg

2 cloves garlic, minced

2 shallots, minced

1 tbsp. olive oil

Salt and pepper

2 cups Fabio's Tomato Sauce (see recipe on page 18)

Fresh parsley, chopped, for garnish

Extra-virgin olive oil, for drizzling

TIP: Don't waste expensive cuts of meat on meatballs! If prepared correctly, a cheaper cut of meat like beef shoulder/chuck, or even scraps will work perfectly.

BRAISED VEAL SHANKS WITH MY GRANDMA'S GREMOLATA

Ossobuco della Nonna

Serves 6

This is a recipe from Milan, in northern Italy. Even though that's not where we were from, we used to make it a lot. My grandma and grandpa were very close to the local butcher. He would give them bones, and around bones there is meat, and if you have shank bones, you're gonna have an osso buco. It's a great recipe—slow and low. Serve it with the Saffron Risotto on page 103.

Mix all the gremolata ingredients together in a bowl and place the bowl in the refrigerator.

Preheat the oven to 325°F.

Season the shanks on all sides with salt and pepper.

Heat the oil in a Dutch oven and sear the shanks over medium heat until browned. Remove the shanks from the pan and set aside.

Add the wine to the pan, scraping the bottom to loosen and dissolve any brown bits. Once the wine is reduced by half and there are no brown bits stuck on the bottom of the pan, remove the reduction from the heat and drizzle it over the shanks.

Return the pan to the burner and add the butter. When it has melted, add the onions, carrots, celery, garlic, and all the herbs. Sauté until the vegetables are softened, about 10 minutes, then turn the heat up to high and add the beef stock and the tomato sauce.

Add the veal shanks and juices, evenly distributing them in the pan. Bring the liquid to a simmer, then cover the pan with aluminum foil perforated in a few spots to release steam, and place it in the oven. Cook for about 2 hours.

About halfway through, turn the shanks over in the pan and place it back into the oven. The shanks are cooked when the meat falls easily off the bone when pulled with a fork. If the sauce is still too watery, remove shanks from the pan, set aside, and reduce the sauce to desired thickness on the stove.

Serve with about 1 tablespoon of gremolata on top of each portion.

For the gremolata:

1 cup parsley, finely minced

4 small to medium cloves garlic, very finely minced

½ cup lemon peel, finely minced

¼ cup capers, finely minced

1 tbsp. extra-virgin olive oil

For the veal:

6 veal shanks, 10–12 oz. each

Salt and pepper

4 tbsp. olive oil

3 cups red wine

3 tbsp. butter

2 medium red onions, diced small

3 carrots, peeled and diced small

3 stalks celery, peeled and diced small

10 medium cloves garlic

3 bay leaves

10 large sprigs fresh rosemary

5 sprigs parsley

3 cups beef stock (see page 263)

2 cups Fabio's Tomato Sauce (see page 18)

When I was eleven, my mom developed a problem with her hands. She was in great pain and had to quit her job. She needed a lot of surgery, and I decided to find a job, because there was no money. When it was raining outside, I had to wrap my shoes in plastic bags because I had the cheapest ones you could buy. They were fabric with cardboard soles, and if they got wet, they would split open. I hated to go out in the rain because other kids would make fun of me with my feet wrapped in bags. My father was working three jobs already, a twenty-hour day, and I was old enough to say, "I've got to change this."

Through odd jobs I was doing, I met a guy who told me he was looking for somebody to work at night. He said nobody wanted the job— it was unloading fifty-pound bags of flour and baking pies from one in the morning until seven. All I wanted to know was how much it paid, and when he said $600 a week, I said, "That's $2400 a month—I want the job!" He wondered what my family would say, so I talked to my dad who said, "I don't like you working at night but I know how you are, and you'll do it anyway. So just don't tell your mother."

My dad told me to tell my mom that during the week I wanted to stay at my aunt's house, three blocks away. My aunt was only seventeen, and she lived with my mom's parents and older sister. It was a perfect plan. The only people who

knew about it were my aunt, my grandpa, and my dad. But the job was forty miles away and there was no bus at one in the morning, so my grandpa said, "We'll do this: You can use that motor bike over there every night as long as it's back by eight and you don't take it before midnight." (Like I said—Mafioso Nonno.) So that was what I did. I "borrowed" this motorbike every night and I never even knew whose it was. Taking it was actually the least illegal thing I was doing, because you have to be fourteen to drive a motorcycle, not to mention to go to work.

I did that job for two and a half years, from one in the morning until seven. The bakery had a nice storefront but there was a basement down some outside stairs, and that was where I worked. There were twenty double-decker ovens down there, blasting heat. My job was to get raw pies from the store, take them outside and down the steps into the basement, bake them, then take them back upstairs—outside again— and into the store. Finally, I'd arrange them on the shelves so everything was fresh for the morning.

The constant change in temperature made me sick every other week, and still I went to work. I spent my nights on the steps, sitting in the middle of the staircase. Ten feet up it was ten degrees, ten feet down it was one hundred and twenty. It was so hot and damp in the basement that I would wait for the pies to bake wearing nothing but my underwear. Then I'd put on a jacket over

> *My mom is the best thing in the world. And like most moms, she would kill anybody on the spot if she believed that for some reason that person was against her son.*

my underwear, check for people in the street, go up the stairs to get into the store with the pies, back and forth again and again. This went on for four to five hours a night. The first two hours of every night I spent helping this big guy unload fifty-pound bags of flour from his truck into the store. My back would be killing me—I was eleven years old! Eventually my mom found out because of all my aches and pains, and all she could say was, "You're going to kill me with this, but thank God you're helping." So I kept doing it because I made $600 a week and it kept my family fed. To this day, when I see an apple pie my back hurts and I sweat and get hot flashes.

Of course, working all night made it hard to stay awake in school. I got suspended once because I was sleeping in class, and my mom stormed into the principal's office when she found out I wouldn't be able to go to school for a week (I wasn't too upset, as you can imagine). She dragged me with her and said things to him I can't repeat in a family cookbook. She also said, "You suspended my son? Do you know what he does all night? He's working all night to help our family, standing on his feet from one to seven in the morning, and you suspended him? What do *you* do all day?" She was like a beast, screaming, "My kid is going to be at school every day or we have a problem here!" My mom is the best thing in the world. And like most moms, she would kill anybody on the spot if she believed that for some reason that person was against her son.

SEAFOOD

Il Pesce e' Morto

CH.06

When we were waiting to eat fish for dinner in my family, we would always ask, "How is the fish, Grandma?" And she would always answer, "The fish is dead"—"*Il pesce e' morto.*" She never knew how she was going to cook it until she saw what Grandpa brought from the grocery store and the garden. Maybe with wine sauce, maybe with tomato, maybe with herbs. But we always knew for sure that the fish was dead.

Fish, of course, is different from seafood. You can't call something that comes from a lake seafood. I'd be offended if I was a fish— "I'm a small-town river carp, not a huge ocean tuna!" If you want seafood in Florence, you drive about two hours to the city of Viareggio, which is on the coast. All along the harbor where the fishing boats dock, you'd see washing machines. If you heard a *thump thump thump* sound coming from them, you knew it was a good day to catch octopus.

Octopus is a very tough animal because it has so much muscle, so what people would do, including us, was go fishing for octopus and then put them in these washing machines with some seawater and some small rocks and tumble them for about an hour until they were tender. The machines always had about twenty-five extension cords that probably led to somebody's apartment up on the third floor, so we'd use a machine and then pay the guy who owned it a few lira (equal to about two American dollars). After an hour in the washing machine, the octopus was so tender it cooked in less than an hour on the stove. Luckily for you, you can just get your seafood at the fish market instead of driving two hours. You can also tenderize it without a washing machine. Just put it in a plastic bag inside another plastic bag and pound it. It's not necessary, but it will make the octopus much more tender for eating (though I've never eaten octopus here that was anywhere near as tender as what I remember from those trips to Viareggio).

FRIED SEAFOOD WITH HERBS AND BURNT LEMON

Paranza

Serves 4

Place all the seafood in a bowl with the buttermilk and soak for about 1 hour.

While the seafood is soaking, combine the flour, salt, and pepper on a plate. Heat the oil over medium heat in a deep sauté pan (the heavier the better).

When the oil is ready, prepare the seafood for frying. Place each piece on the plate of flour and roll it with your hand to make sure it's fully coated. Let the pieces sit for a minute or two so they really absorb the flour.

When the seafood is all floured, turn the heat under the oil up to high and fry the seafood in small batches. Remove each piece to a plate covered with parchment paper as it becomes crisp.

With the last batch of seafood, add the herbs, garlic cloves, and thin slices of lemon to the oil. Watch out for spattering, and keep an eye on the herbs as they will cook and become crispy faster than the fish. When they do, remove them from the oil immediately.

Serve using the fried herbs as a bed for the seafood, with the lemon slices arranged around it.

4 whole squid (about 1 lb.), cleaned, tentacles separated, bodies sliced in half, then cut in strips

1 cup shrimp, shelled and deveined, tail on, heads on or off as you prefer

10 whole sardines or other small fish about 3–5 inches long, like fresh anchovies or small perch

1 cup buttermilk

2 cups flour

3 tsp. salt, plus more for seasoning

1 tbsp. pepper

3 quarts olive oil

A large handful of fresh thyme sprigs

1 small bunch rosemary

10 cloves garlic, skin on

3 lemons, 1 sliced into rounds, the others cut into wedges

DRUNK CURED SALMON

Salmone Ubriaco

This makes a great appetizer served with bread.

Rinse the salmon under cold running water and pat it dry. Place it skin-side down on several large sheets of plastic wrap.

In a mixing bowl, combine the salt, sugar, dill, grappa, and lemon, lime, and orange zests. Spread the mixture evenly over the fleshy side of the fish, pressing it into the fish with the palms of your hands.

Wrap the salmon tightly in the plastic wrap and place it skin-side down on a sheet pan. Now you need to put some weight on it. If your grandma is small enough to fit into the fridge, have her sit on the salmon for 48 hours. If she is not up for it, then put another sheet pan on top of the salmon and weight it with some dishes or heavy tomato cans for 36–48 hours.

Unwrap the salmon and rinse off the curing mixture under cold running water. Pat dry and slice diagonally into paper-thin slices.

1 2-lb. salmon fillet, boneless, skin on
½ cup salt
3 tbsp. brown sugar
¼ cup fresh dill, chopped
¼ cup grappa
2 tbsp. lemon zest
2 tbsp. lime zest
2 tbsp. orange zest

STEWED SWORDFISH

Spada al Sugo

This dish and the tuna recipe that comes next are very similar. The fish are both very meaty and both are cooked in a marinara sauce, one on the stove and one in the oven, with different ingredients. The secret here is to prep the sauce ahead of time.

Preheat the oven to 400°F.

In a medium sauté pan, heat 3 tablespoons of olive oil over medium-high heat, then add the onion, olives, and garlic and cook until golden brown. Add the tomato puree and the cherry tomatoes and keep cooking until the sauce is bubbling. Season with salt and pepper. Turn off heat.

Heat the remaining 3 tablespoons of oil in another sauté pan. Season the fish with salt and pepper, then coat each steak with the chopped herbs and fry in the oil over high heat until the herbs start to brown a bit, about 2 minutes per side. The inside of the fish will still be raw.

Pour the tomato sauce into an ovenproof dish, put the fish on top of it, and cook in the oven for about 10 minutes to cook the fish through. Serve very hot.

6 tbsp. olive oil

1 small red onion, thinly sliced

1 cup black olives, pitted and cut in half

5 cloves garlic, smashed

2 cups canned tomato puree

2 cups cherry tomatoes, cut in half

Salt and pepper

4 swordfish steaks, about 6 oz. each

2 tsp. fresh oregano, finely chopped

2 tsp. fresh basil, finely chopped

TUNA WITH TOMATOES AND CAPERS

Tuna alla Livornese   Serves 4

Place the garlic in a deep sauté pan with the bunches of oregano. Add the oil, turn the heat to medium, and cook until the garlic starts to turn golden.

Add the anchovies, mashing them with a wooden spoon. Then add the rosemary and the tomato sauce and bring to a boil. Turn the heat down a bit and reduce for 10–15 minutes, then add the capers and the cherry tomatoes and season with salt and pepper if necessary.

Place the tuna steaks into the sauce and cook on each side for about 5 minutes over medium heat. Turn the heat off and let the fish rest for 10 minutes.

Remove the tuna and serve with the sauce (reduce it more if you like) and with fresh parsley on top.

6 cloves garlic, crushed

2 bunches oregano, tied with string

½ cup olive oil

8 anchovy fillets

2 sprigs rosemary

2 cups Fabio's Tomato Sauce (see recipe on page 18)

½ cup capers, drained, or rinsed if salted

2 lb. cherry tomatoes, cut in half

Salt and pepper

4 tuna steaks, 8 oz. each, preferably center cut

Fresh parsley, chopped

GRANDMA'S CANNED TUNA

Tonno all'Olio

Serves 4 as an appetizer

People in Italy don't really eat canned tuna. I mean, if you need to make a quick sandwich with mayonnaise and capers because you're headed to a soccer game in twenty minutes, sure. But otherwise tuna from the fishmonger that you poach yourself is tastier and cheaper. We had a lot of tuna at certain times because our next-door neighbor was from Sicily and once a year he would drive down there and bring back the best tuna you ever had after the *mattanza*, when fishermen go out in four or five boats and form a circle around huge nets that catch tons of tuna. It's a little bit violent to see, but the result is you get fresh tuna on your table and that's what it's all about. Tradition sometimes is not polite, tradition sometimes is not politically correct, but it's tradition and you can't really argue with that. In Italy we have a lot of yellowfin and albacore tuna and those are amazing tuna to make this dish with. It's like out-of-control canned tuna.

1 sprig rosemary

1 sprig sage

2 bay leaves

3 cloves garlic, smashed

½ lemon, sliced

4 albacore tuna fillets, 6 oz. each, cut into 2-inch cubes

2 cups olive oil

2 tsp. salt

1 tsp. black peppercorns

Put the rosemary, sage, bay leaves, garlic, and lemon slices in a deep saucepan. Arrange the tuna on top and pour in the oil to cover the fish. The pan should not be too wide or the fish won't be covered.

Cook over low heat for about 10–12 minutes. When the first few bubbles appear in the oil, it's time to turn the heat off.

Flip the fish cubes and place a lid on the pan. Let it sit for about 20 minutes, then drain the oil and season with salt and pepper.

It will keep for about 10 days stored in oil in an airtight container in the refrigerator.

WHERE IS THE FISH? (WHOLE FISH BAKED IN SALT)

Un c'e il Pesce

Serves 6–8

You can make this dish with a big fish, but we could never afford a big, meaty fish, so we had a lot of little fishes or fish pieces. My mom would bring them to the table and my dad would say, "Oh, we have salt-crusted fish. But where is the fish?"

The salt crust acts almost like a steam chamber, so the fish is perfectly steamed and stays moist and juicy. Serve this at the table, breaking open the salt in front of your family to show off. Try to lift off the top of the salt crust in one piece for maximum effect. My dad always crushed the salt and looked stupid, but my mom and I were masters at it. My dad has chubby fingers and was not able to sneak one underneath the salt. You have to be gentle.

Preheat the oven to 425°F and set the rack in the middle.

Place the herbs, lemon slices, and mustard seeds into the fish cavity. Then rub the skin with some of the olive oil and place the fish onto a baking sheet or into a pan.

Combine the egg whites, salt, pepper, and lemon zest in a bowl and mix with your hands until all the salt has been moistened.

Cover the whole fish with the salt mixture, starting with the body and then covering the head and the tail if you have enough salt left over.

Bake the fish for 20–40 minutes, depending on its weight. It should take about 10 minutes per pound of fish.

Transfer the fish to a platter and serve by breaking the salt crust and filleting. To remove the fish correctly—and most dramatically—chip the edges of the salt crust, gently lift the salt off the top of the fish in one large piece, then lift the whole fish out of the salt.

Serve with a drizzle of extra-virgin olive oil.

1 whole fish, about 3 lb., such as sea bass, red snapper, loup de mer, or sea bream, gutted, scales on or off

A few sprigs of fresh herbs (basil, parsley, rosemary)

2 lemons, sliced

A handful of mustard seeds

3 tbsp. olive oil

5 egg whites

6 lb. salt (2 lb. of salt for every 1 lb. of fish)

1 tbsp. pepper

2 tbsp. lemon zest

Extra-virgin olive oil, for drizzling

WHOLE FISH WITH FENNEL-PEPPER CRUST

Pesce al Finocchio e Pepe Nero

Serves 2–3

Preheat the oven to 400°F.

Make 4 diagonal slices about ½-inch deep on each side of the fish. Salt and oil the fish generously.

In a mortar or a spice grinder, combine the fennel seeds and pepper, then coat the outside of the fish with the mixture. Place the lemon and garlic in the cavity.

Cover the bottom of a baking dish with foil, making sure there is enough to wrap around the fish, and spread the herbs on the foil as a cushion for the fish. Place the fish on top and pour the wine around the fish and on the herbs, making sure that the wine doesn't wash off the fennel-pepper coating.

Wrap the foil loosely around the fish, creating a tent, and bake for about 30–35 minutes.

1 whole fish, about 2–3 lb., such as snapper or bass, gutted, scales off

Salt

¼ cup olive oil

2 tbsp. fennel seeds

2 tbsp. pepper

8 lemon slices

6 cloves garlic, smashed

2 bundles assorted fresh herbs, such as thyme, marjoram, and oregano

2 cups dry white wine

FISH BALLS IN TOMATO WINE SAUCE

Polpette di Pesce

Put the olive oil and shallot in a sauté pan and cook for about 5–6 minutes over medium heat. When the shallots start to caramelize, about 5 minutes, add the garlic. When the garlic is golden brown, about 3–4 more minutes, add the pine nuts, the paprika, and the fish. Season with salt and pepper and keep cooking until the outside of the fish is completely cooked and has turned opaque.

Remove the fish mixture from the pan and place in a medium bowl to cool down for 5 minutes. Then add the oregano, rosemary, parsley, breadcrumbs, Parmesan, egg and egg yolks, lemon zest, and lemon juice to the bowl and mix with a spoon or your hands to combine.

Moisten your hands with olive oil and shape the fish mixture into small balls, roughly golf ball–size. Place them on a plate and refrigerate for about 1 hour.

Preheat the oven to 375°F.

When the fish balls are cool, place them in a baking dish and bake for about 15 minutes, then remove from the oven and set them aside to cool for about 20 minutes.

While they're cooling, heat the tomato sauce over medium heat, then add the stock and cook for about 5 minutes until the liquid has reached a medium boil. Add the fish balls, mix, and turn the heat off.

Serve with fresh chopped parsley and a drizzle of extra-virgin olive oil.

4 tbsp. olive oil

1 shallot, finely minced

2 cloves garlic, finely minced

½ cup pine nuts

2 tsp. paprika

1 lb. meaty white fish such as halibut, tilapia, or cod, finely diced

Salt and pepper

1 tsp. fresh oregano, minced

1 tsp. fresh rosemary, minced

2 tbsp. parsley, chopped, plus more for serving

1½ cups breadcrumbs (see recipe on page 275)

½ cup Parmesan cheese, grated

1 egg plus 2 egg yolks

1 tbsp. lemon zest

2 tbsp. lemon juice

2 cups Fabio's Tomato Sauce (see recipe on page 18)

1 cup of fish or shellfish stock (see recipes on pages 261 and 262)

Extra-virgin olive oil, for drizzling

ROASTED MUSSELS WITH LEMON-WINE SAUCE

Cozze al Forno

Serves 4 (or me and Grandpa alone)

Preheat the oven to 325°F.

In a large Dutch oven with a lid, heat the olive oil over medium heat. Add the shallots, garlic, and red pepper flakes and cook until tender and lightly caramelized.

Add the wine and cook over medium-low heat for about 15 minutes, until it is reduced by half. Add the stock and the lemon juice. Taste and season with salt and pepper if needed.

Add the mussels and the parsley and mix everything well. Cover the pot, and cook in the oven until the mussels open, about 5–7 minutes (they're ready as soon as they open). Discard any that do not open.

2 tbsp. olive oil

2 shallots, halved and very thinly sliced

2 cloves garlic, thinly sliced

½ tsp. crushed red pepper flakes, or more to taste

1 cup dry white wine

1 cup fish stock (see recipe on page 261)

2 tbsp. lemon juice

Salt and pepper

4 lb. mussels, scrubbed

½ cup parsley, chopped

BRAISED OCTOPUS

Zuppa di Polpo

Heat the olive oil in a large Dutch oven. Add the garlic and stir over medium heat for about 2 minutes.

Add the octopus, and let it sizzle for about 10 minutes until the skins start to burst a little bit, then add the tomatoes, wine, parsley, bay leaves, red pepper flakes, and olives. Turn the heat to low, cover, and cook for about 1½–2 hours, stirring periodically, until the octopus is tender.

Season with salt and pepper to taste, then add the capers and garnish with fresh chopped parsley. Serve over thick slices of toasted bread.

⅔ cup olive oil

10 cloves garlic, crushed

3 lb. small octopus, cleaned

3 cups canned or boxed tomatoes, drained and diced

2 cups red wine

½ cup parsley, chopped, plus more for serving

5 bay leaves

1 tsp. red pepper flakes

1 cup black olives, pitted and sliced

Salt and pepper

½ cup capers, drained or rinsed if salted

Bread, toasted, for serving

SEAFOOD CIOPPINO

Zuppa di Pesce

Cioppino is just whatever-fish-you-have stew. This is a very simple, inexpensive version, but if you want to make more of a full meal, add some pieces of salmon, some halibut, and some scallops. Pay attention to the cooking time, because if you have fillets you want to add them only for the last five minutes, in pieces no bigger than 1-inch by 1-inch. Steamed rice is also great in this.

Heat the butter in a large stockpot and sauté the onions and leeks with a pinch of salt until translucent. Add the red pepper flakes, bay leaf, and thyme sprigs.

Put the mussels and clams in the pot, give them a stir, then add the wine. Cook until the wine has disappeared, then add the stock.

Bring to a gentle simmer, cover with a lid, and cook for about 10 minutes until all the shells have opened (discard any that have not). Add the squid, shrimp, tomatoes, and cream and let the soup simmer for 5–6 minutes.

Remove from heat, adjust seasoning, and ladle soup into one large bowl to serve family style, or individual bowls if you prefer. Serve with the minced parsley on top.

3 tbsp. butter

1 onion, diced

4 leeks, rinsed well and sliced into thin rounds

Salt

¼ tsp. red pepper flakes

1 bay leaf

2 sprigs thyme

20 mussels, scrubbed

20 clams, scrubbed

¼ cup dry white wine

3 cups chicken or vegetable stock, hot (see recipes on page 260 and 264)

1 cup squid, whole or cut in half

1 cup large shrimp (about 8), shelled and deveined, tails on, heads on or off as you prefer

1 15-oz. can whole tomatoes, diced

1 cup heavy cream

¼ cup parsley, minced

SPINACH STEWED CALAMARI

Calamari in Zimino   Serves 4

Place the olive oil into a large pan over medium heat. Add the onions and celery, a pinch of salt, and some pepper. Cook until the onion is caramelized, about 10 minutes.

Add the tomatoes, spinach, another pinch each of salt and pepper, and the baking soda, which will keep the spinach green.

Cover the pot and cook for 20 minutes over medium heat, stirring occasionally to make sure all ingredients are well mixed.

Remove the lid, turn the heat up to medium high, and add the squid. Cook uncovered for 10 minutes, stirring from time to time.

When the squid has turned white and the spinach has released all of its water, adjust for salt and pepper. Remove from heat and serve on thick slices of toasted bread with parsley on top.

1 cup olive oil

2 yellow onions, finely diced

1 celery stalk, chopped

Salt and pepper

12 oz. canned tomatoes, drained and chopped or smashed with your hands

1½ lb. baby spinach

½ tsp. baking soda

1 lb. whole squid, cleaned and cut in half

Bread, toasted, for serving

2 tbsp. parsley, minced

One morning when I was working at the bakery, one of our regular clients came in. He wanted to know what I was doing there so early, and when I told him I was working, he asked how old I was. I said I was thirteen. He asked if I liked working at night, and I said, "No, I hate it, but what can I do?" He told me if I ever wanted a day job, he owned a small restaurant around the corner called *Il Pallaio* where I should come see him. I went right away. The man's name was Simone, and that was the beginning of my real culinary education. He taught me everything I know about being successful.

Right after I started working at *Il Pallaio*, I turned fourteen and graduated from middle school. I enrolled at a culinary institute where we did regular schoolwork for part of the day and culinary school for the rest of it. I wasn't interested in math or history or anything but the here and now. I also missed a lot of school because I was working so much, and that was what I really cared about. When I bothered to go to school at all, I went for the first part of the day and then went to work in the afternoon until about one or two in the morning.

Il Pallaio was the most important place in the world to me. It was a classic Italian restaurant. It was small, it was all wood inside, the kitchen was old and beat up, and the bathroom smelled like mildew, but the place did some of the most amazing food I ever had in my life. All the basics were there, and I learned absolutely everything. The restaurant was closed Mondays and Tuesdays, so even when I was still in school, every Sunday night I either got on a train or, once I was old enough to drive, into a car and went to restaurants in different cities thanks to Simone's connections. In each of them, I spent time mastering the cooking techniques and cultures of other regions in Italy, like Emilia-Romagna, Piedmont, Lazio, Liguria, Campania, Sardinia, Sicily, and Puglia.

I worked at *Il Pallaio* nonstop for years. I managed to graduate from culinary school when I was eighteen, but only by bribing the teachers with wine and food I'd bring from the restaurant. Basically, they passed me in order to get rid of me! I never took a day off work unless the restaurant was closed, and I loved it. Then, when I was nineteen, the head chef got drunk and somehow put a huge butcher knife through the palm of his hand. Simone said, "We've got to find somebody else to run the kitchen. Who can we

It's true: Less is more. Sometimes when you overdo it, you lose it.

find? Who can we find?" I told him I would do it and he kept saying, "Fabio, you can't do it." Once again I announced, "I got this!" And I did, and that was it. When the chef came back, Simone said, "I gave your position to Fabio." I was doing everything—running the restaurant, doing inventory, and writing the weekly specials. It was the first time I managed a full-blown kitchen.

Even though I was in charge, I wasn't really in charge. Rita was in charge. Rita ran the prep kitchen in the mornings, and she was old when I was young. She's probably ninety by now and she's still working there, and I bet she's still eating as much as she's prepping. It didn't matter what time I got there in the morning because whenever it was, she was already there. I'd get to

work at six in the morning, and she was there. So then I'd get there at five, and she was there! I'd say, "How? Why?" And she'd say, "Because you have to learn, and I'm here to teach you. You're a good kid but you have to take it down about a thousand notches. Just relax and enjoy the ride. And when you come here at five because you know we have a busy day, you're going to see me here at four. If you come at four, I'll be here at three. And if you decide to come here at two in the morning, I'll sleep in the walk-in refrigerator overnight." She was like my business great-grandmother.

Rita was always upset with me because I would take basic stuff and make it fancy and weird. She would say, "Less is more. Less is more. Less is more. You gotta talk less, listen more. Less is more. Don't add all this sauce. Less is more. Don't add all those garnishes, less is more. Don't squeeze too much lemon, less is more." And I would say, "I hate less is more! I hate it!" But it's true: Less *is* more. Sometimes when you overdo it, you lose it.

Rita did what she wanted, whenever she wanted, for as long as she wanted. She had the key to the restaurant, not to mention the restaurant's checkbook, and the vendors would do anything she asked them to. Every day, someone would bring her something. She got whole cases of wine for free. "Rita! It's so good to see you! Why don't you retire? Here's a case of Brunello!" And I was like, "Guys, what about Fabio? I'm here every day. Don't you see me? I've been here for

Il Pallaio *was the most important place in the world to me. It was a classic Italian restaurant. It was small, it was all wood inside, the kitchen was old and beat up, and the bathroom smelled like mildew, but the place did some of the most amazing food I ever had in my life.*

years! What about a salami for me or something?" They always ignored me. So even when I was running the kitchen, she was running the kitchen. I remember once I got really mad at a server and I yelled at him, "Unless Rita is here, I'm in charge!" He just stared at me because it came out so naturally he and I both knew it was the truth.

With Rita, there was never a recipe. This was how our conversations in the prep kitchen went:

"Rita, how many carrots?"

"A few more."

"How many more?"

"A few more!"

"Like a handful more, a cup more?"

"A few more carrots. You have to look at it. You have to feel it. Listen to it."

"What are you talking about? How do you listen to carrots?"

She was like common sense embodied, and she was that way with everything. Try to bake a cake without a recipe! She did it every day. She wasn't related to anybody at the restaurant, but we called her "Mamma Rita." No one knew where she came from because you'd ask her and she'd always say, "It doesn't matter. How's the food?"

CHICKEN

I' Pollo

CH. **07**

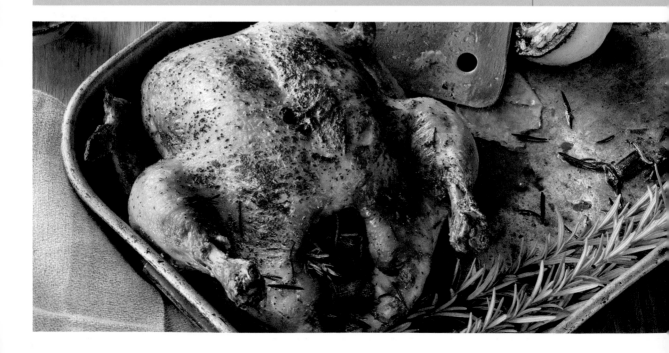

Do you want 365 eggs to feed you for one year, or a chicken to feed you for one day? When you have that kind of power in the household, you're a happy bird.

The chickens my family owned were pretty lucky chickens, because we needed eggs more than we needed to eat chicken. The math was simple: Do you want 365 eggs to feed you for one year, or a chicken to feed you for one day? When you have that kind of power in the household, you're a happy bird: Unless we saw you were limping or old, you were going to live—and live well, because sooner or later you'd be food for my family and me.

When we did finally want to eat chicken, my grandpa would kill one and give it to my grandma. After cleaning it (and keeping the neck, liver, heart, and feet for other recipes), she would marinate the whole chicken in herbs and olive oil for at least half a day. Then she'd cut it up and roast it in our wood oven until the skin was really crispy and the meat was super juicy. You, I hope, are not cooking with a wood oven in your kitchen, so the recipe for Grandma's roasted chicken on page 177 is made in a regular oven.

The chickens were also my friends. When I misbehaved (never!), my mom would call the old phone my grandpa had in his garden shed. She was the only one who knew the number, so they didn't even need to talk. If he heard it ring, he knew to start walking to meet us halfway between my house and the land where he had his garden and the chicken coop. My mom would hand me over to him, and he would take me back to the field. Then he would send me out to play with the chickens.

SWEET AND SOUR CHICKEN WINGS

Ali di Pollo

Serves 4–6

Preheat the oven to 350°F.

Season the chicken wings on all sides with the flavored salt, then coat them with flour, shaking off any excess.

Heat the olive oil in a large skillet over medium heat and brown the wings on both sides. Transfer the chicken to a bowl.

Combine all the remaining ingredients in a sauté pan and reduce by half on medium heat, about 10 minutes. Make sure to break up the anchovies so they dissolve.

Add the sauce to the bowl with the chicken wings and toss them to coat well. Bake in a Pyrex dish for 30 minutes, turning the wings over halfway through.

2 lb. chicken wings, cleaned

2 tbsp. Aromatic Flavored Salt (see recipe on page 276)

½ cup flour

2 cups olive oil

1 cup honey

½ cup vinegar

2 cloves garlic, minced

2 anchovy fillets

¼ cup orange juice

⅓ cup ketchup

1 tsp. lemon juice

HEN WITH
SAGE-GARLIC SAUCE

Gallina alla Salvia

Serves 4–6

Cut the chicken into 8 pieces. Mix the garlic and ⅔ of the sage leaves in a bowl.

Place the oil and butter in a medium-size Dutch oven over medium heat. When the butter has melted, put the chicken pieces into the casserole and sauté for 4–5 minutes on each side, or until just golden all over. Add the garlic-and-sage mixture and sauté for 5 more minutes. Add the wine and cook over high heat for 10 more minutes. Season with salt and pepper.

The meat should be half-cooked at this point. Add 1 cup of the stock and keep cooking, adding more stock in small amounts until the chicken falls off the bones at the touch of a fork and the stock is reduced completely.

Adjust for salt and pepper, then transfer the chicken and its sauce to a large serving platter and serve with the rest of the sage leaves.

1 large chicken (3 lb. or more)

15 cloves garlic, finely chopped

2 bunches sage, leaves only

6 tbsp. olive oil

2 tbsp. butter

2 cups dry white wine

Salt and pepper

About 1–2 cups chicken stock (see recipe on page 260)

FRIED ROSEMARY CHICKEN

Pollo Fritto

I know. Nobody in my family is from the American South. But we have some mean fried chicken in Italy. This chicken is so good that if I opened a chain restaurant that served only fried chicken tomorrow, Popeyes and Kentucky Fried Chicken would have to start making pancakes for a living. For the best chicken, you should let it marinate overnight in the refrigerator. But if you're pressed for time, a few hours is enough.

In a dish large enough to hold all the chicken, mix together the buttermilk, 4 sprigs of the rosemary, and the garlic. Add the chicken, cover, and let marinate anywhere from a few hours to overnight in the refrigerator.

Mix 3 cups of the flour with the paprika, pepper, and mustard powder in a rectangular dish large enough to dredge the chicken. Drain the chicken from the buttermilk, and roll the wet pieces in the flour mixture.

Heat the oil in a deep sauté pan. While it is heating, coat the lemon slices with the remaining ¼ cup of flour and set them aside.

Fry the chicken for 8–10 minutes, turning it to get even color. Then add the remaining rosemary sprigs, the sage, and the floured lemon slices to the oil and fry the chicken, herbs, and lemon for another 7–10 minutes.

Remove the chicken from the oil and drain on paper towels. Season with salt and pepper, if desired, and serve with the fried lemon wedges and herbs.

---

3 cups buttermilk

8 sprigs rosemary

8 cloves garlic, crushed

1 whole chicken, cut into 10–12 pieces

3 cups plus ¼ cup flour

2 tbsp. smoked paprika

2 tbsp. pepper

1 tbsp. mustard powder

3 cups olive oil

1 lemon, sliced thin

3 sprigs sage

Salt and pepper

[Fried Rosemary Chicken] is so good that if I opened a chain restaurant that served only fried chicken tomorrow, Popeyes and Kentucky Fried Chicken would have to start making pancakes for a living.

CHICKEN WITH MARSALA SAUCE

Pollo al Marsala   Serves 2

Melt the butter in a nonstick pan over medium heat. Add the thyme and let it heat through, then add the garlic and the sliced mushrooms. Season the entire pan with salt and pepper and cook until the mushrooms begin to brown and crisp, about 5 minutes.

Meanwhile, pound the chicken breasts with a mallet until they are about ½-inch thick. Dredge each chicken breast in flour and shake off the excess.

Heat the olive oil over medium-high heat in a separate nonstick pan. Add the floured chicken breasts and cook them for about 2 minutes on each side. Add the wine to the pan and let it start to reduce, then add the mushroom, garlic, and thyme mixture to the chicken pan, along with the heavy cream. Cook over medium heat until the cream has reduced and thickened. Remove the chicken from the pan and serve topped with the remaining sauce.

2 tbsp. butter

1 sprig thyme

3 cloves garlic, smashed

1 cup oyster or shiitake mushrooms, sliced

Salt and pepper

2 boneless, skinless chicken breasts

2 cups flour

1 tbsp. olive oil

1 cup sweet Marsala wine

¼ cup heavy cream

CHICKEN HUNTER STYLE

Pollo alla Cacciatora

Serves 3–4

You can do this with a whole chicken or you can use thighs or drumsticks, as in this recipe—whatever you want. Why hunter style? A hunter goes into the forest and he steps on mushrooms, and at least in Italy, hunters drink red wine. When I used to go hunting with my grandfather, he would bring a flask of wine that could knock out an army, but in this dish there's just a little wine to deglaze the pan. Feel free to add more stuff—more herbs, white onion instead of red, anything earthy and woody. Add different kinds of mushrooms. If you grow zucchini in the forest behind your house, add some zucchini. I don't mind! This is just a basic recipe.

In a sauté pan over medium-high heat, combine 4 tablespoons of the oil with the onion, garlic, mushrooms, olives, and rosemary sprigs and a pinch of salt and pepper.

Cook until caramelized, about 5 minutes, then turn the heat down to low and add the thyme sprigs. Turn off the heat.

Generously coat the chicken pieces with flour. Heat the remaining 4 tablespoons of oil in another sauté pan over medium-high heat and sear the chicken pieces until crisp on all sides.

Add the chicken and all pan drippings to the pan with the vegetables. Then deglaze, adding the wine and the tomato sauce (see page 21 for a tip on deglazing.)

Cover with a lid and cook over medium-high heat until the chicken is done, about 15 minutes.

8 tbsp. olive oil

1 red onion, roughly chopped

5–6 cloves garlic, crushed

2 cups fresh mushrooms, roughly chopped

1 cup of your preferred olives, pitted and sliced (I like black)

2 sprigs rosemary

Salt and pepper

4 sprigs thyme

6 pieces dark-meat chicken, bone in (thighs and drumsticks)

1–2 cups flour

2 cups red wine

2 cups Fabio's Tomato Sauce (see recipe on page 18)

GRANDMA'S ROASTED CHICKEN

Pollo della Nonna

Serves 2–4

Grandma's roasted chicken is the recipe that made me who I am on American television, even though I broke my finger waiting for my turn to start the challenge in the *Top Chef* semi-finals. Because I've never found chef's shoes that were comfortable, I was wearing sneakers for the show and I slipped. I put my hand out to break my fall, so I wouldn't crack my head on the floor, and my whole finger went back and the knuckle popped out. But I stood back up, I fought on, I made my grandma's roasted chicken, and I won. It's the juiciest chicken you'll ever have, because Grandma didn't have a lot of teeth left so dry chicken was not an option for her. Follow the recipe for the ultimate roasted chicken.

1 whole chicken, 2–4 lb.

¼ cup olive oil

Sea salt and pepper

5–6 cloves garlic, crushed

1 lemon, sliced

2 sprigs thyme

2 sprigs sage

2 sprigs rosemary

Extra-virgin olive oil, for drizzling

Preheat the oven to 450°F.

Remove the organs, gizzards, and neck from the chicken and rinse it inside and out with cold water.

Pat the chicken dry with paper towels so that the oil and seasonings will stick. Rub olive oil all over the skin and season heavily with salt and pepper. Stuff the cavity with the garlic, lemon, and herbs.

Place the chicken in a roasting pan, breast-side up, and put it into the oven. Roast for approximately 15–20 minutes, until the skin is crispy and brown.

Put a meat thermometer in the breast, turn the chicken over so it is breast-side down, and turn the oven down to 350°F. Continue roasting until the thermometer reads around 150°F. Then turn the oven off and let the chicken stay in the hot oven until the thermometer reaches 160–165°F.

Cut the chicken into legs, drums, wings, and breasts, place the pieces on a platter, drizzle with extra-virgin olive oil, and garnish with the roasted thyme, sage, and rosemary.

CHICKEN PICCATA

Piccata di Pollo

Serves 4

Piccata means "pounded" in Italian. In America, chicken piccata is associated with a lemony caper sauce, but that's not the only way you can make it. My family's traditional chicken piccata is with mushrooms, like the chicken Marsala recipe above, but it can also be made with lemon, or with red wine and radicchio, or with whatever the heck you want. But unless you *piccata* it, don't call it *piccata*.

Place each chicken piece between two sheets of plastic wrap and pound, using a meat mallet, to a thickness of about ¼ inch.

Heat 1 tbsp. of the butter and the olive oil in a sauté pan over medium heat.

Season the chicken on both sides with salt, pepper, and paprika. Cook in the olive oil until nicely browned on both sides.

Add the ½ cup of lemon juice, the stock, the capers, the rest of the butter, and the lemon slices. Reduce until the sauce is thick and velvety. Turn off the heat.

Julienne the radicchio and toss it in a bowl with the 2 tablespoons of lemon juice, the Parmesan, and the extra-virgin olive oil, plus a pinch of salt and pepper.

Serve the chicken with the radicchio on top.

4 boneless, skinless chicken breasts, cut in half lengthwise into 8 flat, even pieces

3 tbsp. butter

1 tbsp. olive oil

Salt and pepper

1 tbsp. paprika

½ cup plus 2 tbsp. lemon juice

¼ cup chicken or beef stock (see recipes on pages 260 and 263)

4 tbsp. capers, drained, or rinsed if salted

1 lemon, sliced into ⅙-inch rounds

3 whole radicchio Treviso (the long one)

2 cups shaved Parmesan cheese

2 tbsp. extra-virgin olive oil

Piccata *means pounded in Italian. But unless you* piccata *it, don't call it* piccata.

DRUNKEN CHICKEN

Pollo Ubriaco

Normally, drunken chicken has red wine but mine uses white wine with a little lemon and garlic: My family didn't really like white wine for drinking, so we always had some left over. It's a very simple dish but the zest of the wine gives it an amazing flavor, especially if you use something dry like a Chardonnay or a Pinot Grigio.

Season the chicken with salt, pepper, and paprika, then dust it with flour. Heat the oil in a deep sauté pan, add the oregano, and brown the chicken on all sides, about 10–15 minutes. Remove the chicken from the pan and set aside.

Add the onions to the pan with the chicken drippings and season with salt and pepper. Cook over medium heat, and when the onions begin to caramelize, add the garlic and cook until it is golden brown.

Add the wine to deglaze the pan, scraping up any brown bits stuck to the bottom with a flat wooden spoon. (See page 21 for a tip on deglazing.) Put the chicken back in.

Add 1½ cups of the chicken stock and the tarragon and bring the mixture to a boil on high heat. Reduce the heat to a simmer, cover the pan, and cook, turning the chicken pieces over a few times, until cooked through, about 30 minutes. The meat should come off the bone easily when pulled with a fork. If necessary, add more stock as the chicken cooks to keep it from drying out or frying.

Take the chicken out of the pan again. Remove the tarragon sprigs and add the remaining tablespoon of flour. Whisk the sauce until it has no lumps.

Put the chicken back in the pan and cook for 2 more minutes.

---

1 whole chicken, cut into
8 pieces
Salt and pepper
1 tsp. paprika
1 tbsp. flour, plus extra for
dusting
½ cup olive oil
1 tsp. dry oregano
1 lb. pearl onions, trimmed
and peeled
6 cloves garlic, halved
3 cups white wine
1½ cups chicken stock,
plus a bit more on hand
just in case (see recipe
on page 260)
2 sprigs tarragon

While I was working at *Il Pal-laio*, I was dating a woman eleven years older than me named Erica. I chased her for years when I was a kid, and I finally won her over when I was eighteen. She was the first woman I ever cooked for in a romantic way and she was the one who made me realize I needed to forget high-end cuisine, get down and dirty, and teach everybody how to make simple food. Erica and fancy food were like the moon and the sun—two completely different planets. One day, after I had made dinner for her, she said, "Fabio, this is great but I don't know what I'm eating. I need a plate of pasta. I'm hungry! I love that you're so passionate and you're trying to make all these fancy dishes, but let's make some *food* here! We're at home." I had completely forgotten about "Less is more."

I went back to my family basics for her. We often made the pici recipe in this book, and the salt-crusted fish. She loved the pumpkin risotto with walnuts, too. Because of her I changed my beliefs about what good food is. I realized that if you satisfy yourself, you only increase your ego, but if you satisfy a lot of people, you make everyone happy *and* you create more business.

Unfortunately, all the business my new approach brought also led to me making a big mistake by not marrying her. My grandpa always told me to find one woman and spend the rest of my life with her, and I should have taken his advice with Erica because she was the perfect person. But it was the wrong time. I was too obsessed with my work, and she left me after I was so scared to break up with her I got Rita to call her up and persuade her to break up with me. And then she went off with a soccer player. I don't know if it's a curse on me or not, but the women in the three most important relationships I had in Italy all ended up with soccer players. Luckily, the person I'm with now loves me very much and doesn't care about sports at all. Also, soccer is not a big deal in America, so I don't need to worry.

Near the end of our romance, Erica and I planned a trip to Paris. When it looked like things were finally over, I invited my best friend since birth, Tommaso, to come along to Paris instead. It was going to be my first vacation in years. Two days before we left, Erica convinced me we should give things one more try. I told Tommaso and said I hoped he understood. He said, "Don't worry about it. I'll go visit my mom for a few days instead."

I went to Paris with Erica and he went to his mother's house. The second night, he got up because he wasn't feeling well. He was having trouble breathing, and he went to wake up his mother. Then he passed out and he was already in a coma when the ambulance came. He died on his way to the hospital.

I wished I hadn't gone on the trip to Paris. I wished I'd taken my best friend rather than

catching lizards in the countryside around Florence, where there were tons of them. We'd take a broken fishing pole, tie a little loop at the end of it, and challenge each other to sneak up on a lizard and get it in the loop. Then we'd compete to see who could catch more lizards.

One day, when we were about fourteen, we caught hundreds of lizards this way. We were lizard maniacs! We had some Lego bricks and we built a lizard house with little Lego windows you could open and close, and we filled it up with lizards. We were so excited about how many lizards we had captured that we decided to go show them to my mom. We walked into my kitchen and she said, "What do you guys have there?"

"We have a lot of lizards!" we announced, and then we accidentally dropped the house full of lizards. Maybe twenty lizards landed on the table, and roughly another hundred went running off in every direction. My mom was finding dead and live lizards for a year after that. In the bathroom. In the beds. I had a cat and he was going bananas. My mom said, "No more lizards. You guys are fourteen! Go play soccer!"

After that, we gave up lizard hunting, but we couldn't give up lizards entirely. Instead, we went out and got one lizard each tattooed over our hearts. When Tommaso died, I got a second lizard tattooed next to my first one in his honor, so even though Tommaso is gone, the memory of what we did together will always be with me.

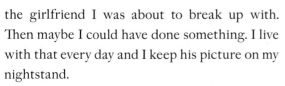

the girlfriend I was about to break up with. Then maybe I could have done something. I live with that every day and I keep his picture on my nightstand.

When Tommaso and I were kids, one of the ways we wasted time and had some fun was

SALADS & VEGETABLES

Insalate e Contorni

Fried Fresh Mushrooms 188 | Fried Squash Blossoms 190 | Dirty Cabbage with Pork 190 | Broken Potatoes with Burnt Lemon and Parmesan 191 | Eggplant Caponata 193 | Roasted Old Ladies (Roasted Vegetables) 194 | Cauliflower Stewed with Tomato 196 | Baked Onion Gratin 197 | Leeks Tucked in Bed with Prosciutto 199 | Baked Stuffed Tomatoes 201 | Red Wine Poached Pear Salad 202 | Arugula Salad with Sundried Tomatoes and Mushroom 203 | Tuna and Lettuce Salad 203

In Italy, if you put salad on the steak plate, I'll know for sure that you are not Italian!

Eating vegetables and salad at my house wasn't always the happiest moment in the day, because we just had to take whatever we could get from my grandpa's garden. I don't remember ever seeing my mom come home with a bag of butter lettuce or a bag of tomatoes. If it grew in our garden, we ate it. If it didn't grow, we didn't waste money on it.

We had some pretty good vegetable dishes, but they weren't the stars. It was more like, "We have this, this, and this, and oh, some veggies." We never said, "Let's have a salad for lunch!" My grandpa would have thrown a nightmare fit! I think that's fairly typical for Italian culture. In Italy, you will hardly ever encounter anyone who is willing to sit down in front of a bowl of salad and call it a meal. If we want to eat lighter, we eat less pasta, less meat, less fish. Vegetables are a side dish.

In America, salad is leafy and crunchy—lettuce, cucumbers, tomatoes. In Italy, salad can get very creative, and you eat it *after* your main course (not before, because before is when you have cold cuts and pasta). Salads are more like full side dishes—artichokes, beets, carrots, asparagus, turnips. They're dressed with nothing but extra-virgin olive oil, salt, and red wine vinegar, and you don't eat them on the same plate as the entrée; you serve them on their own plates. In Italy, if you put salad on the steak plate, I'll know for sure that you are *not* Italian!

FRIED FRESH MUSHROOMS

Funghi Fritti   Serves 4

We never had a lot of mushrooms, so we cut them in pieces and breaded them so it seemed like more. You can do this with all kinds of mushrooms, but I suggest oyster or porcini mushrooms.

Cut the mushrooms into slices about ½-inch thick or, if the mushrooms are small, leave them whole. Place them in the sparkling water or 7-Up to soak for about 20 minutes. While they are soaking, put the flour in a shallow open container. Take the mushrooms out of the liquid and, without drying them, toss them in the flour until they are well coated all over.

Once coated, let the mushrooms rest for about 25 minutes on a paper towel to make sure that the coating will stick to them. In the meantime, heat the olive oil to 350°F (see page 107 for a tip on how to use a wooden spoon to check whether your oil is ready) in a large sauté pan over medium-high heat.

Place the mushrooms carefully into the hot oil, making sure not to crowd them, along with the rosemary. Fry until the batter is crispy and light brown and the slices are hard to the touch, about 3–5 minutes per side. Then take them out and place them on a paper towel to drain (unless you're in my family, where there's not enough time to put them on a towel before they're all eaten). If you are not quite ready to serve them, you can put them on parchment paper rather than a paper towel to prevent them from getting soggy. Season them with salt and pepper right away. Remove the rosemary sprigs from the oil, too, and when they have cooled enough to touch, break them apart all over the mushrooms.

Serve immediately with a few lemon slices if you want. The best crispy mushroom, period.

1 lb. fresh oyster or other wild mushrooms
3 cups sparkling water or 7-Up
1 cup flour
3 cups olive oil
3 sprigs rosemary
Salt and pepper

BROKEN POTATOES WITH BURNT LEMON AND PARMESAN

Patate Rotte

Serves 6

Put the oil in a large sauté pan over medium heat.

With the palm of your hands, crush the potatoes enough for the skins to burst but not enough to make them fall apart. Put the potatoes into the oil and cook until crisp on one side.

Add the rosemary and the garlic and turn the potatoes over to crisp the other side. Total cooking time for crisping both sides will be about 15 minutes. (Remember: The skin needs to be crisp but not burnt. There is a difference between brown and black, right?)

Once crisped, put the potatoes in a bowl and toss them with the rest of the ingredients except the lemons.

To serve, put the potatoes on a platter and squeeze the lemons on top.

2 tbsp. olive oil

2 lb. baby potatoes, boiled in water for 5 minutes then shocked in ice water and patted dry

½ cup fresh rosemary, roughly chopped

2 cloves garlic, minced

1 good pinch of salt

Lots of pepper

1 cup Parmesan cheese, grated

A handful of chives, chopped

4 halves Roasted Lemons (see recipe on page 25)

Caponata

Serves 4

Everybody loves sweet-and-sour flavor. Now, we almost always put eggplant in caponata, but the traditional caponata was made with whatever vegetables were left over from the field, braised in vinegar and sugar to take the unfresh flavor away. The original Sicilian caponata doesn't include carrots, but my mom makes it with carrots. My grandma does it without carrots. And I do what I like. If you have carrots, put some in; if you don't have carrots, don't worry! This is a good side dish, but it's also good as a topping and as an appetizer. You're going to get a standing ovation when you serve this even on plain bread.

In a large Dutch oven, combine the celery, carrots, and onion with the olive oil. Cook over medium heat until the vegetables are nicely caramelized, then add the garlic and cook for another 3 minutes.

Next add the eggplant, tossing and stirring the chunks as they heat up to help them absorb all the oil. Once they've released a bit of water, turn the heat to high and keep stirring. After about 10 minutes, the eggplant will start to get softer and will be reduced in size. Then add the capers, olives, and pine nuts, and cook for another 5 minutes.

Add the brown sugar and the vinegar, and as soon as the vinegar has reduced add the tomato sauce mixed with the tomato paste. Cook for another 10 minutes and add the basil. Season with salt and pepper. Turn the heat down to medium and cook until the tomato sauce is completely reduced and there is no trace of water left.

Remove from heat and let rest for about 30 minutes. Serve with lemon zest and mint on top.

1 cup celery, diced

1 cup carrots, diced

1 large yellow onion, diced small

1½ cups olive oil

5 cloves garlic, crushed (not minced)

3 large eggplants, half the skin removed in strips with a vegetable peeler, cut into 1-inch chunks

½ cup capers in water, drained

1½ cups pitted green olives, sliced

1 cup pine nuts

2 tbsp. brown sugar

½ cup red wine vinegar

2 cups Fabio's Tomato Sauce (see recipe on page 18) mixed with 2 tbsp. tomato paste

1 bunch basil, leaves only

Salt and pepper

Zest of 1 lemon

Mint leaves for garnish

ROASTED OLD LADIES (ROASTED VEGETABLES)

Vecchie al Forno

Serves 6

In the summertime, we used to get tons of veggies from my grandpa's garden, and sometimes we had a lot left over. When you have too many carrots to eat in a month, the carrots at the bottom of the bucket become all wrinkled, and it's the same with beets and eggplant. Just as Grandma has some wrinkles, the vegetables have wrinkles, too, so we used to call them roasted old ladies.

Preheat the oven to 450°F.

Whisk the balsamic glaze and the olive oil in a bowl large enough to hold all the vegetables. Add the garlic, oregano, basil, and salt and pepper to taste and whisk again.

Discard the seeds of the peppers and cut the peppers into 4 pieces lengthwise.

Toss all the vegetables into the bowl with the dressing and let them sit for about 30 minutes, mixing every once in a while. Distribute them into 2 baking dishes and roast for about 15–20 minutes or until the edges are golden brown.

Remove and serve with the extra-virgin olive oil and the lemon breadcrumbs on top.

2 tbsp. balsamic glaze (see recipe on page 268)

½ cup olive oil

3 cloves garlic, smashed with a garlic press

3 tsp. fresh oregano, finely chopped

3 tsp. fresh basil, finely chopped

Salt and pepper

1 yellow bell pepper

1 red bell pepper

1 green bell pepper

2 large red onions, sliced in rounds

2 skinny or Japanese eggplants, quartered lengthwise and cut in half again

3 zucchini, cut into ⅓-inch-thick rounds

3 carrots, cut into 4 pieces lengthwise

3 tbsp. extra-virgin olive oil

1 cup breadcrumbs mixed with the zest of 2 lemons (see recipe for bread-crumbs on page 275)

CAULIFLOWER STEWED WITH TOMATO

Cavolfiore al Pomodoro

Serves 4

Preheat the oven to 350°F.

Parboil the cauliflower for 5 minutes in salted water, then shock it in an ice bath (see note below for how to make an ice bath).

Put the oil into a large pan with the garlic and pine nuts and cook over medium heat until the garlic becomes translucent. Add the cauliflower, stirring it gently to turn it over.

After cooking for about 10 minutes, add the tomato sauce and stir. Season with salt and pepper.

Place into a baking dish and top with the Parmesan or ricotta. Bake in the oven for about 25–30 minutes. Serve piping hot.

NOTE: To make an ice bath, fill a large bowl about halfway with ice, then add water to cover the ice while still leaving enough room to place a smaller bowl, a filled Ziploc bag, or whatever else you're cooling into it without causing an overflow.

1 large cauliflower, cut into florets
3 tbsp. olive oil
10 cloves garlic, crushed (or minced for a little more garlic flavor)
1 cup pine nuts
1 cup Fabio's Tomato Sauce (see recipe on page 18)
Salt and pepper
1 cup Parmesan cheese, grated, or 1 cup ricotta cheese

BAKED ONION GRATIN

Torta di Cipolle

Serves 6–8

Preheat the oven to 375°F.

Put the oil and butter in a large sauté pan and turn the heat on medium low. Once the butter foams, add the garlic and the onions. Stir and cook until well caramelized. Do *not* let them burn.

Add the cream and the vinegar and reduce until the onions are completely coated. The mixture should look like syrup. Remove from heat and set aside.

Beat the eggs, then combine them with the Gruyere and the onion mixture. Season to taste with salt and pepper. Divide evenly between the 2 prebaked pie crusts.

Place the pies on baking sheets, sprinkle them with Parmesan, and place in the oven. Bake for 15–20 minutes, or until the filling is set and starting to brown.

2 tbsp. olive oil

6 tbsp. butter

5 cloves garlic, sliced

2 lb. red and white onions, sliced

½ cup heavy cream

⅔ cup balsamic vinegar

3 eggs

1 cup Gruyere cheese, grated

Salt and pepper

2 9-inch pie crusts, prebaked (or use tart recipe from page 40)

1¼ cups Parmesan cheese, grated

LEEKS TUCKED IN BED WITH PROSCIUTTO

Porri a Letto

Serves 6–8

My mom used to call these leeks "tucked in bed" as a way of making me be quiet. Whenever we had leeks, she'd make the dish and then say, "Do you want to help me tuck them in?" I'd help her tuck in the prosciutto and then she'd say, "Now you have to be quiet because the leeks are sleeping." Then I would go around the house telling everyone, "Be quiet! The leeks are sleeping!"

8 leeks, cleaned
½ cup olive oil
1 tsp. salt
1 tsp. pepper
1 tbsp. mustard
1 tbsp. balsamic glaze (see recipe on page 268)
2 cups Pecorino cheese, grated
20 slices prosciutto

Preheat the oven to 350°F.

Cut the top 2 inches off the leeks (the green part), and chop each leek into 3 equal parts. Blanch them for about 10–12 minutes in boiling salted water, remove from water and let them cool down to room temperature.

In a large bowl, mix the olive oil, salt, pepper, mustard, and balsamic glaze. Add the leeks and toss them to coat.

Arrange the leeks in a baking dish, standing up on their ends like soldiers, close together. Cover the leeks with the Pecorino, then lay the prosciutto over the cheese, tucking the slices under the bottoms of the leeks so they are fully covered.

Bake for about 30 minutes or until the prosciutto starts to get really crispy. Remove from the oven and, using a sharp knife, cut off one corner for a dramatic presentation.

You make kids happy,
and you make Mom
happy. Everybody wins.
Except the tomato,
of course.

ARUGULA SALAD WITH SUNDRIED TOMATOES AND MUSHROOMS

Funghi e Pomodori

Serves 4

3 cups arugula

3 tbsp. extra-virgin olive oil

1 tbsp. balsamic vinegar

1 tbsp. white wine vinegar

1 cup sundried tomatoes, cut into strips (see recipe on page 24)

1 cup button mushrooms, sliced very thin with a mandoline

Salt and pepper

10 basil leaves

Flesh of ½ cantaloupe, scooped out with a melon baller

Toss everything in a large bowl and serve family style!

TUNA AND LETTUCE SALAD

Lattuga e Tonno

Serves 4

1 recipe Grandma's Canned Tuna (see recipe on page 148), shredded with a fork

1 head butter lettuce, roughly chopped

2–3 tbsp. extra-virgin olive oil

1–2 tbsp. red wine vinegar

Salt and pepper

2 scallions, thinly sliced

Parmesan cheese flakes

Olives (if you want—my Grandma always did)

1 cup cannellini beans (optional)

Green beans, blanched (optional)

Place all the ingredients in a salad bowl and toss well to mix.

DESSERTS

I' Dolci di Casa Viviani

Fabio's Cake 208 | Apple Cake with Grappa 211 | Fabio's Mom's Tiramisu 212 | Ricotta Chocolate Chip Fritters 215 | Grape Tart 216 | Fluffy Chestnut Milk Pancakes 217 | Roasted Apples with Ricotta, Hazelnuts, and Chocolate 218 | Strawberries with Red Wine 219 | Poached Pears with Ricotta and Balsamic Vinegar 220 | Cooked Cream with Red Wine Syrup 223 | Basic Meringue 224 | Ugly But Good Cookies 227 | Basic Gelato (Don't Call It Ice Cream) 228 | Lemon Sorbet 231 | Perfect Holeless Doughnuts 233 | Caramel Nut Crunch 234

Many people think of dessert as a last impression—a chance to wow their guests one last time. But we're Italian! We don't need to do that, since we impress people with every part of the meal. We invented wowing!

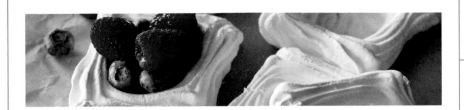

Many people think of dessert as a last impression—a chance to wow their guests one last time. But we're Italian! We don't need to do that, since we impress people with every part of the meal. We *invented* wowing!

The desserts here are very traditional, but the way I make tiramisu is not the way someone from Milan does it. These desserts are done the way I do them. You can find another Italian who will say, "No, the fritters need to have walnuts!" To that I say, "Well, sure, add what you like. But not in my house!"

In my family, after we had eaten our entrée we would lick the plate or do *scarpetta* by getting a little piece of bread and wiping the surface of the plate practically dishwasher-clean with the mushy white part of the bread. Then we would turn the plate upside down and be ready for dessert.

FABIO'S CAKE

Torta di Fabio

This is really a 101 cake. If you can make this, you can call yourself a pastry chef—you just made a cake! Also, I happen to know that the Pope likes it (see the Introduction for that story)! It has the same texture as rice pudding but it tastes like apple, and it's perfect to have your kids make at home with you.

Preheat the oven to 350°F.

Beat the eggs and sugar until foamy in a stand mixer with a paddle attachment. Add all the remaining ingredients except the butter and flour and mix until everything is incorporated.

Grease and flour a 9-inch round springform baking pan. Pour the batter in and bake for 1 hour. For a crunchier crust I sometimes sprinkle a bit of brown sugar on top before baking.

Eat! This cake is also perfect dried out after a week, with a glass of cold milk.

2 eggs plus 1 egg yolk
¾ cup sugar
1 cup flour
½ cup olive oil
2 tsp. baking powder
1 tsp. vanilla extract
Zest of 1 orange
3 cups very ripe apples, peeled, cored, and crushed
Butter and flour for the pan

APPLE CAKE WITH GRAPPA

Torta di Mele e Grappa   Serves either me and my grandpa or 6 normal people

Preheat the oven to 375°F.

To make the crust, place the dry ingredients and the orange zest in a food processor, turn it on, then add the eggs and the cream. When they are incorporated, turn off the food processor, add the butter, and pulse till the dough looks unified but still lumpy. Some little butter pieces should still be visible (this will make the crust flaky).

Remove the dough to a cool surface and, using your hands, form it into a ball. Wrap the ball in plastic wrap and put it in the fridge to chill for 10 minutes.

When it has chilled, place the dough on a floured surface and roll it out into a circle large enough to cover the bottom and sides of a 10-inch springform pan with about ½ inch hanging over the side. Place the dough into the pan and then in the fridge to rest while you prepare the apple filling.

To make the filling, slice the apples in sixteenths and put them in a bowl with the orange juice to prevent them from discoloring. Put the walnuts and grappa together in a bowl and toss the walnuts to make sure the grappa really soaks in.

Take the pan with the prepared dough from the fridge and layer the walnuts on the bottom. Then remove the apple slices from the orange juice and layer them on top of the walnuts (don't add any of the leftover juice).

To make the topping, mix all the ingredients except the egg whites in a bowl. Then beat the egg whites to a medium peak in a separate bowl and fold them into the mixture. Spread over the cake top, pressing down a bit with a plastic spatula. Fold the dough hanging over the sides of the pan over the topping to form a border of about an inch all the way around the cake and bake for about 30–40 minutes or until the top and the pastry are nicely browned.

For the crust:

1½ cups flour, plus extra for dusting your work surface

A pinch of salt

¼ tsp. baking powder

½ cup sugar

1 tsp. orange zest, finely grated

1 egg

3 tbsp. heavy cream

12 tbsp. (1½ sticks) butter, *very* cold

For the filling:

4 Red Delicious apples (or other varieties that are not too hard or too tart), peeled and cored

Juice of 1 orange

½ cup walnuts, chopped

4 tbsp. grappa

For the topping:

½ cup brown sugar

3 tbsp. butter, melted

1 tbsp. grappa

1 tsp. baking powder

2 tbsp. heavy cream

2 egg whites

FABIO'S MOM'S TIRAMISU

Tiramisu della Mamma di Fabio

Serves 4–6

Buy a box of ladyfingers for this recipe. If you have any left over, they're fantastic soaked in milk the next morning. If you buy a big box, the best part of the recipe is you know you will have ladyfingers for breakfast.

In a medium bowl, beat the egg yolks and sugar with an electric mixer until light and fluffy. Either fold in the mascarpone or use the electric mixer on low to mix it in. Place the mixture in the fridge for about 30 minutes, until it is set.

Meanwhile, pour the cold coffee into a mixing bowl and add the vanilla extract. When the mascarpone mixture is ready, spread it in a thin layer on the bottom of a 6 x 9-inch baking dish.

Dip the ladyfingers one by one very quickly into the coffee, then lay them onto the mascarpone mixture. Repeat until the mascarpone is covered. With a cheese grater, shave some of the chocolate on top of the ladyfingers. Repeat the layers, starting again with the mascarpone, until the dish is full. The top layer should be mascarpone with chocolate grated over it.

Serve immediately or keep chilled in the fridge for later.

1 pot strong coffee (about 3 cups), chilled

12 egg yolks

½ cup granulated sugar

2 lb. mascarpone cheese, at room temperature

1 tbsp. vanilla extract

30–35 ladyfinger cookies

1 chunk dark chocolate, large enough for grating

Once a month, you are allowed to stuff your face with ricotta and chocolate fritters. It's the perfect substitute for a bottle of whiskey when you have had a very bad week.

RICOTTA CHOCOLATE CHIP FRITTERS

Fritelle di Ricotta

Makes about 15 fritters

I'm not even going to talk about this one. These fritters are too good to be talked about. You just have to make them, eat them, and don't say anything to anyone. I know the recipe says "makes about 15 fritters," but who cares? Sit down, beg for forgiveness first, then eat them all, feel guilty about it, pray, pay your dues, and do it all over again next month. Once a month, you are allowed to stuff your face with ricotta and chocolate fritters. It's the perfect substitute for a bottle of whiskey when you have had a very bad week. Not that I endorse drinking to forget.

1 lb. ricotta cheese

½ cup mini chocolate chips

3 tbsp. flour

1 quart olive oil

Sugar for dusting

Mix the ricotta cheese, mini chocolate chips, and flour in a bowl until well combined.

Pour the oil into a large sauté pan and place over medium-high heat.

Using 2 spoons, scoop the ricotta mixture into slightly flat football-shaped fritters and place them carefully into the hot oil. Let the fritters cook until they are crisp and brown on the outside.

Using a slotted spoon, pull the fritters out of the oil one by one and put them on a paper towel to drain. As they cool, dust them with sugar.

Crostata di Uva

I learned how to make this tart at the nameless deli where my grandpa and I took our grapes to have them pressed for wine. While we did the *vendemmia*—stomping on the grapes—the woman who worked there would make pie crust. When we were done, there were always a lot of partly crushed grapes left over, so she'd put them in pies and we'd take them home with our fifty gallons of juice for wine. This very simple, straightforward dessert will wow all your guests.

Preheat the oven to 375°F.

Butter and flour the bottom and sides of an 8-inch round springform pan.

To make the crust, place all the crust ingredients except the butter into a food processor. Pulse about 10 times, then add the butter and pulse till incorporated. Do this quickly or the crust will fall apart in the oven. Wrap the dough in plastic wrap and refrigerate for at least 1 hour.

To make the filling, whip the egg whites in a bowl until they form a medium peak (you should be able to turn the bowl upside down without the egg whites falling out) and put them aside. Place the rest of the filling ingredients except the grapes into a food processor and combine by pulsing. Remove and fold the whipped egg whites gently into the mixture.

Place the chilled dough between 2 sheets of plastic wrap and roll it out to about ¼-inch thick, so it will fit into your buttered, floured pan. Place the dough in the pan so it covers the bottom and a little bit of the sides of the pan.

Crush the grapes a bit with your hands and put them onto the crust dough, then pour in the filling and spread it evenly. Bake in the middle rack of the oven for about 1¼ hours or until the top and the pastry are browned.

Remove the tart from the oven, dust the top with graham cracker crumbs, and allow it to rest for 15 minutes. Serve at room temperature.

For the crust:

2¼ cups unbleached flour

⅔ cup superfine sugar

3 egg yolks

Peel of 1 lemon, grated

Pinch of salt

10 tbsp. (1¼ sticks) butter, cold and cut into pieces

For the filling:

2 egg whites

4 egg yolks

¼ cup flour

1 tbsp. Grand Marnier, or any orange liqueur

1 cup heavy cream

½ cup brown sugar

1 lb. seedless red grapes, stems removed

½ cup graham crackers, finely crushed

FLUFFY CHESTNUT MILK PANCAKES

Necci

Come on, America, you don't need an Italian to teach you how to make pancakes! Just cook them until they're brown.

Mix the eggs, egg yolks, and milk in a large bowl, then add the flour a little at a time until it is all incorporated. Mix in the honey and the 3 cups of ricotta.

Heat about 1 tablespoon of the olive oil in a nonstick pan over medium heat and use a ladle to put about 2 tablespoons of batter into the oil. Rotate the pan with your wrist to spread the batter into a thick disk shape, and fry until nicely browned. Flip to the other side and cook for 1 more minute. Put the pancake aside and repeat, adding more oil and batter for each pancake.

Spread the pancakes with ricotta and top with the crumbled chestnuts to serve.

3 extra-large eggs, plus 3 egg yolks

2½ cups milk

2 cups chestnut flour, sifted

1 cup honey

3 cups ricotta cheese, plus extra for serving

3 tbsp. olive oil

1 cup roasted chestnuts, peeled and crumbled

ROASTED APPLES WITH RICOTTA, HAZELNUTS, AND CHOCOLATE

Mele Ripiene

Serves 6

We always had big chunks of chocolate at my house, and we used to crack little pieces off with a knife and mix them with ricotta and a little bit of hazelnut for this dessert. We had a beautiful hazelnut tree outside my house, and my mom would send me out to pick nuts for this dish. It's so simple, but amazing.

Preheat the oven to 375°F.

Slice a small piece off each apple bottom so they will stand without falling over. Cut the tops off the apples and, using a spoon or small knife, carve out the inside, leaving a thickness of about 1 inch of apple all around. Place the apples in a buttered baking dish.

Mix half of the honey, the ricotta, the orange zest, the hazelnuts, and the chocolate in a bowl and fill the inside of each apple, mounding the top.

Drizzle with the rest of the honey and place in the oven for about 15 minutes or until the top starts to melt and the skin of the apples has colored a little bit.

Serve warm, dusted with powdered sugar.

6 firm baking apples (such as Granny Smith, Pink Lady, Crispin, or Pippin)
½ cup honey, divided in 2
1½ cups ricotta cheese
1 tbsp. orange zest
1 cup hazelnuts, ground or crushed
½ cup dark chocolate, chopped
Powdered sugar for dusting

STRAWBERRIES WITH RED WINE

Fragole Ubriache

Serves 6–8

These strawberries are delicious with a spoonful (or three, like my grandpa used to have) of unsweetened whipped cream. Once you have eaten all the berries, dip some old bread into the wine or just drink it.

Place the fruit in a heatproof bowl or other container.

Pour the wine into a saucepan with the sugar and reduce it to 1 cup over medium heat. Pour the syrup on top of the fruit, then put the mixture in the fridge for about 2 hours to cool.

While it is cooling, make the topping by whipping the cream until firm.

Divide the fruit into bowls and top each one with a dollop of whipped cream to serve.

4 cups ripe strawberries, cut in half, or 4 firm peaches, pitted and sliced in quarters
3 cups leftover red wine
2 tbsp. raw or cane sugar
2 cups heavy cream

POACHED PEARS WITH RICOTTA AND BALSAMIC VINEGAR

Ricotta all'Aceto e Pere

Serves 4

This is such an easy dish to make. You can add a little sugar or honey to the ricotta if you like. It's a fantastic dessert and very light because there is no flour or sugar. The balsamic glaze is just the icing on the cake—which in this case is not quite a cake, but whatever!

In a large saucepan, combine the wine with the honey and the cinnamon and bring to a boil. Add the pears and simmer them in the wine for about 15 minutes.

Take the pears out and let them cool. Turn the heat up to high under the wine sauce and reduce it to about ⅔ cup. Let the sauce cool and place it in the fridge.

Put a few tablespoons of sauce on each of 4 plates and place a pear on each one. Serve each pear with a few dollops of ricotta and a good drizzle of balsamic glaze on top.

3 cups bold red wine, such as Chianti or Cabernet

½ cup honey

2 cinnamon sticks

4 pears, peeled (Bartlett, Bosc, or any other hard-to-the-touch pear)

4–5 tbsp. ricotta cheese (see recipe on page 24)

8 tbsp. balsamic glaze (see recipe on page 268)

TIP: Ricotta and pears also make great bruschetta.

COOKED CREAM WITH RED WINE SYRUP

Panna Cotta   Serves 6–8

Italians are not very big on using heavy cream in entrées or seasoning sauces and dressings. For us, *panna*—cream—has always been for dessert. You can also serve this dish without the wine syrup if you prefer—or if, as in my house, your grandpa drank all the wine syrup while it was still warm.

Put the gelatin and milk in a saucepan and let it bloom for about 20 minutes. Then add the cream, brown sugar, and pinch of salt.

Bring the mixture to a simmer over low heat, whisking to make sure that the gelatin and sugar are dissolved. Then add the vanilla extract or seeds and whisk one more time.

Transfer the cream mixture to a bowl and place the bowl in an ice bath (see note on page 196) for about 30 minutes to cool it down and help it thicken. Divide the mixture into 6-8 glasses and refrigerate for a minimum of 4–5 hours, preferably overnight.

To prepare the wine syrup, place all the ingredients in a saucepan and bring to a boil. Reduce the liquid over medium heat to about ⅓ and cool it completely. Remove the orange peel.

Serve the individual glasses of panna cotta with about 2 tablespoons of wine syrup drizzled on top of each.

For the cream:

3½ tsp. gelatin powder or 6 sheets of gelatin

2 cups whole milk

2 cups heavy cream

6 tbsp. brown sugar

Tiny pinch of fine salt

1½ tsp. vanilla extract or the seeds of 1 vanilla bean (see note below)

For the wine syrup:

3 cups red wine

½ cup sugar or ½ cup honey

1 cinnamon stick

3 ribbons orange peel

NOTE: To use a whole vanilla bean, cut the pod in half lengthwise and use the tip of a sharp knife to scrape the sticky seeds from the inside of the pod.

BASIC MERINGUE

Meringa

Preheat the oven to 275°F.

Line a baking sheet with wax paper.

Beat the egg whites until the whites form firm peaks. You'll know the egg whites are thick enough when you can hold the bowl upside down over your head!

With the mixer still running, add the sugar gradually, then the pinch of salt. Turn the mixer up to its highest setting and beat for about 2–3 minutes. Keep a close eye on the meringue—if you whisk it for too long, it will deflate.

Using a tablespoon, place dollops of the mixture onto the wax paper–lined pan (if you want to be fancy, you can pipe it through an icing bag into squares or other shapes as shown) and bake in the oven for about 2 hours, until the meringues are crisp on the outside and chewy and a little gooey in the middle (they won't spread, so you can put them as close together as you like). Turn off the oven and let the meringue rest there overnight so that it reaches room temperature gradually. If you rush it, the meringue will absorb moisture from the air and will be gooey instead of crisp. Serve crumbled over ice cream, with berries and cream, or just plain with a cup of coffee.

8 egg whites
10 tbsp. superfine sugar
A pinch of salt

UGLY BUT GOOD COOKIES

Brutti ma Buoni

Preheat the oven to 250°F.

Butter and flour a baking sheet.

In a food processor with the blade attachment, finely chop one pile of nuts. Chop the other pile a little bit more coarsely. Combine the finely chopped nuts with ½ the sugar.

Beat the egg whites to a medium peak in a stand mixer with the paddle attachment or in a bowl using a handheld electric mixer, then add the remaining sugar and keep beating until the sugar is fully incorporated. Add the vanilla, honey, cinnamon, and the coarsely chopped nuts, mix to incorporate, and use a flat spatula to transfer the contents of the bowl to a large nonstick pan or enamel casserole. Cook over low heat for 5–10 minutes to dry the dough out a bit.

Using a spoon or an ice cream scoop, form small balls of dough and drop them onto the buttered, floured baking sheet.

Bake the cookies for 35–40 minutes, then raise the oven temperature to 300°F and bake for another 45 minutes or until the cookies are golden brown. Once they look crisp, let them rest on a cooling rack, or forget that and eat them right away, while they are still hot, with milk.

4½ cups blanched hazelnuts, divided into 2 equal piles

Butter and flour for the baking sheet

1 cup sugar

8 egg whites, at room temperature

½ tsp. vanilla extract

½ tbsp. honey

1 large pinch of ground cinnamon

BASIC GELATO (DON'T CALL IT ICE CREAM)

Gelato

Serves 4 (or only Fabio)

If you call Italian gelato ice cream, somebody will come over and slap you in the face. Gelato is not ice cream. It's what ice cream can only hope to be when it dies and goes to heaven. Gelato is thick, rich, and heavy. One gallon of melted gelato is one gallon of liquid, but one gallon of melted ice cream is never one gallon of liquid because it's whipped and filled with air to make it look fluffy and light. When you put a scoop of good gelato in your mouth, it coats your tongue and stays there for a long time before you're ready for your next bite. It's not super easy to make at home, but this version is pretty easy if you have an ice cream maker.

14 egg yolks, beaten
6 cups whole milk
1½ cups sugar
Zest of 1 lemon

In a large saucepan, combine the egg yolks, milk, and sugar. Cook and whisk over very low heat until the custard mixture coats a wooden spoon, about 10–20 minutes.

Add the zest and mix well, then transfer the custard into a large Ziploc bag or a bowl and chill, first in an ice bath then overnight in the fridge. (To make an ice bath, see note on page 196.)

Freeze in a 5-quart ice cream maker according to manufacturer's directions.

[CONTINUED]

NOTE: For this recipe and all the frozen desserts in this section, you'll need to either start the recipe a day ahead or have a whole day during which you can freeze and stir the ingredients.

Gelato is not ice cream. It's what ice cream can only hope to be when it dies and goes to heaven.

VARIATIONS

CHOCOLATE GELATO

Gelato al Cioccolato

Prepare the Basic Gelato recipe without the lemon zest. Instead, add 6 ounces of semi-sweet chocolate to the hot custard and stir until the chocolate is melted. Once the custard has been chilled in an ice bath and the fridge, chop up the rest of the chocolate and whisk it into the mixture. Freeze as directed.

Substitute for the lemon zest:

14 oz. semi-sweet chocolate

PEACH AND MINT GELATO

Gelato alla Pesca e Menta

Prepare the Basic Gelato recipe without the lemon zest. Instead, add the peaches and mint to the hot custard and stir to combine. Chill in an ice bath and the fridge as above and freeze as directed.

Substitute for the lemon zest:

8 ripe peaches, pitted, peeled, and pureed

10–12 mint leaves, hand-torn

LEMON SORBET

Sorbetto di Limone   Serves 6 (if Grandpa is not home)

Put the sugar, water, and vodka into a pan and bring to a boil, then turn the heat down and continue to simmer for 5 minutes.

Once the liquid is clear and syrupy, remove it from the heat and allow it to cool for 15 minutes. When it has cooled, mix it in a glass or ceramic bowl with the lemon juice and zest and place it in the freezer for 1 hour.

Add the mascarpone and stir until completely mixed. Adjust for sweetness if the lemon flavor is too strong, then place it back in the freezer and leave it for at least an hour before you check it.

When it has started to freeze, use a fork to scrape down the sides of the bowl—you can also mix everything a little if you want, though you don't have to—then put it back in the freezer. Repeat as often as possible over the next 24 hours, every hour or so when you're around and awake.

When it has set completely but is still soft—thick enough to hold on a spoon but thin enough to drink out of a glass—enjoy it!

2 cups sugar

2 cups water

3 tbsp. vodka

2 cups lemon juice

Zest of 2 lemons

1 really full tbsp. mascarpone cheese

PERFECT HOLELESS DOUGHNUTS

Bomboloni   Makes 1–2 dozen, depending on size

American donuts have a hole. Italian donuts don't have a hole. Why would you want to eat a bite less? Are you crazy?

Boil the potatoes and allow them to cool before mashing.

Grease 2 baking sheets.

In a stand mixer with the hook attachment, mix the milk, eggs, sugar, and yeast on low for 2 minutes, allowing the yeast to activate. Add the mashed potatoes, then the lard.

Next add 4 cups of the flour, one cup at a time, until it is all incorporated. Add the salt and mix until dough is soft and supple. Remove the dough to a floured surface and knead for 1–2 minutes, adding additional flour if necessary. The dough should be really soft but not sticky.

Roll the dough out to ½-inch thickness. Cut out circles no bigger than 3 inches in diameter with a knife or a pizza cutter and place them on greased baking sheets. Cover with a damp, lightweight towel and let the doughnuts rise until almost doubled in size, about 30 minutes.

In a deep sauté pan, heat the oil to 340°F and cook the doughnuts until they are browned on both sides, flipping them over a few times to get even color.

Remove them from the oil and place on paper towels to drain. If desired, brush the warm doughnuts with melted butter and dip them in powdered sugar.

4 small russet potatoes, about 2–3 cups, peeled and quartered
¼ cup milk, warmed
2 large eggs, lightly beaten
¾ cup sugar
1 package (or 2¼ tsp.) active dry yeast
¾ cup lard
4½ cups bread flour
1 tsp. salt
3 cups olive oil
1 tbsp. butter, melted, plus butter for the pans
Powdered sugar, for dipping

TIP: When frying doughnuts, don't overcrowd your pan. They'll cook more evenly that way because the oil temperature will remain more constant.

CARAMEL NUT CRUNCH

Croccante

Makes 1 sheet pan of candy

This is the perfect treat for your kids. Kids love candy, but candy is 100-percent sugar, so in Italy we give them candy with nutrients in the form of nuts like almonds, hazelnuts, and walnuts! I use regular white sugar, the cheapest I can find, but you can make this with brown sugar, turbinado sugar—all kinds of sugar. If you're a health nut, you can also make this with sesame seeds, quinoa, whole-grain puffed rice, chia seeds . . . whatever you like.

4 cups almonds, skin on
1 cup hazelnuts, skin on
1 cup walnuts, skin on
5 cups sugar
½ cup water

Roast the nuts first to bring out their flavor. In a sauté pan, cook over medium heat until they start to give off a scent.

Place the sugar in a nonstick saucepan and cook over high heat until it starts to melt. If necessary, add a bit of water to help.

Turn the heat down to medium low and continue to cook until the sugar turns a deep rich brown color. Add all the nuts and mix well. Cook for a few minutes, making sure the nuts are fully coated.

Remove from heat and quickly spread the hot mixture onto a cookie mat or an oiled sheet of foil to the desired thickness (I like it about ½ an inch thick).

Let cool for half an hour before breaking it into smaller pieces.

After Tommaso died and my girlfriend left me, I quit the restaurant business for a while. I was in my early twenties and I needed to get some perspective. I'd given my father some money to invest in a tech company he started with a friend of mine, and when the business started getting into trouble, I joined them to try to help it survive. But they were already in too much debt by then, and the company ended up going under. I went back into restaurants to help pay the money back, but I also did it because I missed the work. I lost every dime I had saved in that tech company, but I ended up making it back and then some by building a small empire of restaurants, clubs, and bars in Florence.

But I didn't listen to the main thing Simone taught me back when I worked with him at *Il Pallaio*: "It doesn't matter how good you are, you have to surround yourself with people who are as good or better." He tried to warn me when I was starting out that some of the people I was going into business with weren't trustworthy, but I thought I knew better. My business got too big and was destroyed by unreliable people. Also, Florence is a small city and small Italian cities have a lot of little mafias. That's how I grew up; it is what it is, and you have to deal with it.

People hate your guts if you do well. I once had a gun pointed in my face by someone saying, "If your group takes that storefront, you're going to get hurt." I got beat up just because I'd made

someone angry with my success. When one of my clubs was set on fire, I finally started to understand what was happening. That was when Simone came to me and said, "You've got to get out of here. I guarantee you'll lose everything if you stay in Italy." And for the first time in my life, I listened. My friend Jacopo had moved to California, so I called him up and asked him if he could help me get a job and if I could crash at his apartment. He said yes to both, so in the fall of 2005 I landed in Los Angeles, ready to start over again.

I was about to turn twenty-seven and I had never even been out of Europe. I didn't speak a word of English, and the cultural shock was overwhelming. Everything was big! Cars were big. Streets were big. People would say, "Let's go have a drink," and we'd drive for two hours. What? Two hours? For a drink? In Florence I drive two hours and I'm in Rome! And I would never go as far as Rome for a pizza. I wouldn't have driven two hours to go anywhere. A few other little things that amazed me: People in America take airplanes like they take cabs in my country. And in Italy, when they play the national anthem at a sports event, it's a moment to go grab a beer because the soccer match is about to start. Here, everybody stands with their hand on their heart. It's fantastic, but it was a shock! I will always be too Italian and not American enough for this country, but I love America and its people, too. Now I also stand and sing.

Still, the beginning was tough. Think about this: When I arrived in the United States, it was the end of September. It took me about two months to settle in and learn a bit of English. After that I said, "Okay, I have to grocery shop. I need to learn how to deal." It was the week before Thanksgiving, but I was living with two Italians, and I had no idea about Thanksgiving. So I go to the supermarket. I'm a chef, I know food. I look around and there are turkeys everywhere, and I think, "Wow! This country loves turkey! That's so weird!" The market was all about turkey. So I buy some turkey, I buy some stock. Then I go back about five days after Thanksgiving and there's no turkey anywhere. I thought American supermarkets basically specialized in one ingredient at a time, and all I could think was, "This is crazy. I will be very successful in the U.S. if this is how they run their stores."

Don't even get me started on what it was like trying to date American women before I learned English—of course, I tried! Meanwhile, my mother was writing to me every week to remind me how much she missed me. I'd been living on my own since I was fifteen, but she was used to having me nearby. When I first told her I was moving to America, she thought I was kidding. In her letters, even though she was the same proud, protective mom I'd always known, she couldn't help revealing how sad she was that I was gone. America was a long distance away to her, and there was no money to buy plane tickets for a visit.

But as always, she thought of me before she thought of herself. In one letter, she told me: "Be happy and take care of yourself. My love for you is as big as the sea." Then, she added: "Promise me just one thing: If something is not going right

> *Don't even get me started on what it was like trying to date American women before I learned English— of course, I tried!*

and you don't like it, or if something doesn't go the way you wanted it to, put your pride aside and come back. Here you have a home and a family that adores you." I never thought of moving back, but because of her belief in and love for me, I became the person I am today. Plus, I can finally pay her back for all the stuff I destroyed around the house when I was a kid!

Eventually, by putting away ten Euros a day and taking on extra work, she was able to save up enough money for plane tickets not just for her and my father, but for my grandparents, too. She didn't want me to pay for anyone to visit. When they arrived in Los Angeles nine months after I got there, my mom said it felt like she had carried me in her belly all over again. She couldn't believe she was finally going to see me.

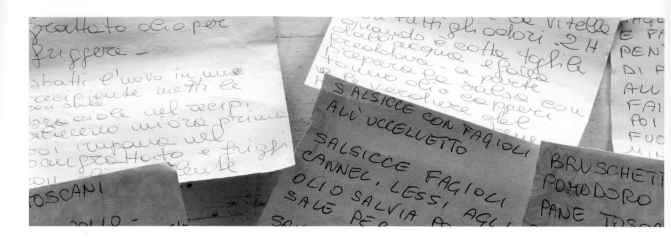

MY MOM'S BRAGGING RIGHTS

L'Orgoglio della Mamma

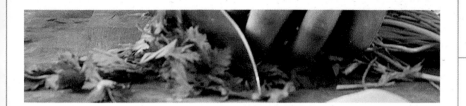

My great-grandma was the chef in our house because my mom had me so young she didn't really have the chance to learn from her mother about the craft of cooking. In some ways that was okay, because the secret in my family was that my mom really didn't like to cook anyway. Still, she couldn't help but learn something from my great-grandma, like I did, and she knew she needed to have some recipes to show off with. After all, we're Italian! These are those recipes, and they were the dishes she was proudest of. They were an exception, but they are still very, very good. Whenever somebody showed up at the house, these were the dishes she made. Or when someone asked, "What do you want to make?" these were her choices—her go-to dishes. These are the dishes that if for some reason she was missing both hands, she'd still find a way to figure them out.

My ultimate favorite among them is the tripe, which is delicious and also brings back great memories for me. So many times my mom would say, "Honey, are you coming home for lunch?" I'd say, "No, Mom, we played soccer and we ate already," and she'd say, "Okay, I'll make some tripe." I'd say it again and she'd still say, "Okay, I'll just make some tripe." And I'd go home after a soccer game on Sunday and have a bowl of tripe with grated Parmesan and hot bread, with my mom.

WHISKEY DUCK PROSCIUTTO

Prosciutto Ubriaco   Serves 6–8

This recipe needs to cure for a week, so plan ahead to make it for a special occasion.

Using a small, really sharp knife, trim the skin and fat to ⅛-inch thickness.

Mix all the remaining ingredients except the whiskey in a medium bowl. Place 2 sheets of plastic wrap side by side on a table.

Place about 1 cup of the seasoning mixture in the center of each sheet, spreading it out so it is just a bit bigger than the size of the duck breasts. Place one duck breast on each piece of plastic wrap, skin-side down on the seasoning mixture.

Spread the remaining mixture over the meat of both breasts, making sure all areas are covered (spread it with your fingers if necessary). Bring the plastic wrap up and over each duck breast, wrapping tightly.

Place the wrapped breasts on a small, rimmed baking sheet, fat-side down, and refrigerate for 6–9 days, depending on the size of the breasts.

Unwrap the duck breasts, wash off the curing mixture with the whiskey, and pat dry. Cut into very thin slices and serve on crunchy bread or just nibble on it.

2 whole boneless duck
  breasts, 1 lb. each, skin
  on
1½ cups salt
1 cup dark brown sugar,
  packed
1 tbsp. pepper
3 bay leaves, crumbled
¼ tsp. smoked paprika
1 tsp. dried rosemary
1 cup whiskey

POUNDED LEMON VEAL

MY MOM'S BRAGGING RIGHTS

P. 243

Scaloppini al Limone   Serves 4

Heat 1 tbsp. of the butter and the olive oil in a sauté pan over medium heat.

Season the veal on both sides with salt, pepper, and paprika. Cook in the oil until nicely brown on both sides.

Add the ½ cup of lemon juice, the stock, the capers, the rest of the butter, and the lemon slices. Reduce until the sauce is thick and velvety. Turn off the heat.

Julienne the radicchio and toss it with the 2 tablespoons of lemon juice, the Parmesan, and the extra-virgin olive oil, plus a pinch of salt and pepper.

Serve the veal with the radicchio on top.

3 tbsp. butter

1 tbsp. olive oil

8 veal cutlets, pounded to about ¼-inch thickness

Salt and pepper

1 tbsp. paprika

½ cup plus 2 tbsp. lemon juice

¼ cup chicken or beef stock (see recipes on pages 260 and 263)

4 tbsp. capers, drained, or rinsed if salted

1 lemon, sliced into ¼-inch rounds

3 heads radicchio Treviso, whole

2 cups shaved Parmesan

2½ tbsp. extra-virgin olive oil

VEAL WITH TUNA SAUCE

Vitello Tonnato   Serves 6

Mix the wine, bay leaves, rosemary, and garlic in a large Dutch oven. Add the veal, then add enough stock to cover the meat. Salt lightly and simmer the meat over medium heat for 1½ hours.

Add the anchovies to the pot and continue simmering for another 15 minutes; the liquid should be reduced by almost half at this point. When the meat is fork-tender, about another 15 minutes, remove it from the pot and strain the broth into a bowl to use later.

Combine the anchovies from the pot with the yolks of the hard-boiled eggs (eat the egg whites or give them to your dog—mine used to love them), plus the capers, tuna, vinegar, lemon juice, and extra-virgin olive oil. Use some of the mayonnaise to dilute the sauce to your taste.

Cut the veal into thin slices and lay them out on a platter. Spread the sauce over the meat, and chill before serving.

1 bottle dry white wine, such as Pinot Grigio

5 bay leaves

1 sprig rosemary

5 cloves garlic, minced

3 lb. veal shoulder, whole

2–3 cups beef stock

Salt

8 salted anchovies

4 eggs, hard-boiled, whites and yolks separated

2 tbsp. capers, minced

1 lb. Grandma's Canned Tuna (see recipe on page 148)

1 tbsp. balsamic vinegar

Juice of 2 lemons

⅓ cup extra-virgin olive oil

1 cup mayonnaise (see recipe on page 270)

TRIPE IN TOMATO

Trippa ai Sugo   Serves 6

Combine the water and vinegar in a large pot and boil the tripe in the mixture for about 15 minutes.

Put the olive oil in a Dutch oven over medium heat. Add the carrots, onion, and celery and cook until the onions are caramelized. Add the garlic and cook for 5 more minutes.

Add the tripe and cook with the vegetables for another 10 minutes or so. Then add the wine and reduce completely.

Add the tomato sauce and the stock, turn the heat to low, and cook until the sauce is reduced and thick, about 1 ¼ hours. The tripe should be very soft and fall apart in your mouth when you taste it.

Season with salt and pepper and serve covered with Parmesan and a killer olive oil.

3 cups water

1 cup red wine vinegar (or any vinegar you prefer)

1 lb. tripe, cleaned and cut into small strips

½ cup olive oil

2 cups carrots, minced

2 cups onions, minced

2 cups celery, minced

5 cloves garlic, minced

1 cup red wine

2 cups Fabio's Tomato Sauce (see recipe on page 18)

1 cup Fabio's stock of your choice (if you pick fish stock, I'll have you arrested)

Salt and pepper

Parmesan cheese, grated

Extra-virgin olive oil, for drizzling

BOILED MEAT WITH GREEN SAUCE

MY MOM'S
BRAGGING RIGHTS

P. 246

Bollito Misto   Serves 8

Combine the water and wine in a very large soup pot and bring to a boil. Season the veal shanks and beef shoulder with salt and pepper and add them to the pot. Return to a simmer and cook for 1 hour, skimming the fat from the top as it cooks.

Add the carrots and celery. Bring to a quick boil and lower the heat again, then add the garlic, onions, rosemary, and sage. Simmer for 1 more hour.

Add the potatoes, chickens, and sausages. Simmer for another hour, continuing to skim the fat.

Set aside 8 cups of the strained broth to serve as a first course. It's very tasty and will keep everyone happy while you finish cooking. Remove the vegetables with a slotted spoon, and serve alongside the meat as is, or topped with flavored oil. Top with fruit mustard and/or green sauce and serve.

TIP: If you reduce the remaining broth, you'll have a knockout flavored stock. *Booooom!*

1 gallon water

3 cups red or white wine

6 3-inch sections veal shank, about 3 pounds

1 piece (about 3 lb.) beef shoulder/chuck

Salt and pepper

1 lb. carrots, cut in half

8 stalks celery, each cut into 2 or 3 pieces

2 cloves garlic

3 medium red onions, halved

2 sprigs rosemary

2 sprigs sage

6 medium potatoes, cut in half

2 small chickens, quartered

4 Italian sausages, cut in half

Flavored oil for drizzling, optional (see recipe on page 274)

½ cup Tuscan Fruit Mustard (see recipe on page 269, or you can buy it, but it won't be as good as homemade!)

⅔ cup Green Sauce (see recipe on page 266)

STEWED COD IN TOMATO SAUCE

Baccala alla Livornese

Serves 6

Season the cod with salt and pepper and coat with flour. Heat the oil in a sauté pan over medium heat and fry the fish, turning, until golden brown and crunchy on the outside.

Place all the other ingredients except the parsley into a deep sauté pan large enough to hold all the fish. Place the fried fish in the middle of the pan.

Cook over medium heat until the stock or water has disappeared, about 15 minutes. Serve with the parsley on top.

6 pieces (4 oz. each) cod, skin off

Salt and pepper

Flour, to coat the cod

2 cups olive oil

2 cups Fabio's Tomato Sauce (see recipe on page 18)

1 red onion, thinly sliced

5 cloves garlic, finely chopped

1 cup green olives, pitted and cut into rounds

1 cup fish stock (see recipe on page 261) or water

½ cup parsley, chopped

EGGPLANT PARMESAN

Melanzane alla Parmigiana

Serves 6–8

Preheat the oven to 425°F.

Heat the oil in a deep sauté pan over medium-high heat. Bread each piece of eggplant by dredging in flour, then egg, then panko. Fry the eggplant in the oil until golden brown, about 2 minutes a side.

Spread a small layer of tomato sauce on the bottom of a square baking dish. Next, layer the sauce with fried eggplant, trimming larger pieces to fit. Top with Parmesan cheese, then shredded mozzarella, then more tomato sauce. Repeat this order for a second layer, then a third layer, adding the basil and oregano on top of the third layer.

The final layer is different: Top the herbs with eggplant, then Parmesan cheese and tomato sauce, and finish with mozzarella. Top with olive oil, salt and pepper.

Bake for 30–40 minutes, then broil for 3–5 minutes until the cheese is brown and bubbly. Remove and let sit for 5–10 minutes before slicing and serving.

2 cups olive oil, plus more for topping

2 medium eggplants, peeled and sliced lengthwise into 1-inch-thick pieces

3 cups flour

6 eggs, beaten

3 cups panko breadcrumbs

1 quart Fabio's Tomato Sauce (see recipe on page 18)

1 cup Parmesan cheese, grated

1 lb. buffalo mozzarella, hand-shredded

1 small bunch fresh basil, leaves only

2 tbsp. fresh oregano

Salt and pepper

MEAT WITH SEVEN FLAVORS

MY MOM'S
BRAGGING RIGHTS

P. 249

Carne ai 7 Sapori   Serves 2

Put the pork into a large bowl and coat the pieces very lightly with flour, salt, and pepper.

Heat the oil in a sauté pan over medium heat and sauté the onions, celery, garlic, and herbs until softened, about 10 minutes. Add the pork and cook until the outside of the meat is no longer pink.

Add the white wine and milk to almost cover the meat. Cook over medium heat until all the liquid is gone, about 15–30 minutes.

Add 2 cups of water or stock and simmer, gradually adding more liquid if needed, for at least 1½ hours. Remove the meat from the pan, and while it is resting, reduce the sauce. Add the capers and hard-boiled eggs—if you are using them—at the end.

Serve with the sauce on top.

1 lb. pork shoulder, cut into 1-inch cubes

Flour, to coat the pork

Salt and pepper

2 tbsp. olive oil

2 onions, finely chopped

4 celery stalks, finely chopped

2–3 cloves of garlic (old garlic is fine), finely chopped

1 tbsp. sage leaves, finely chopped

Bay leaves

1 sprig rosemary

½ bottle white wine, such as Pinot Grigio or Chardonnay

1 cup milk

2–3 cups water or beef stock (see recipe on page 263)

1 tbsp. capers

A few hard-boiled eggs, chopped (optional)

FOUR-CHEESE EGGS

Uova ai Formaggi   Serves 8

We call this four-cheese even if sometimes we only have three.

Preheat the oven to 350°F.

In a saucepan over low heat, melt the butter, then stir the flour in very slowly and cook until golden brown. Add the milk and the cream and cook for about 10 minutes until the sauce has thickened and can coat the back of a spoon.

Remove the pan from the heat and stir in all the cheeses and the paprika. Pour the cheese sauce into a nonstick dish. Once it starts to cool down and set, about 5 minutes, break the eggs into it. Space them out well in the dish to keep them from touching and breaking.

Bake for 20–30 minutes or until the egg whites are opaque and cooked through. Serve on toasted bread with basil on top.

8 tbsp. butter

½ cup flour

4 cups milk

1 cup cream

1 cup Taleggio (or cheddar) cheese, shredded

1 cup Swiss cheese, shredded

½ cup Parmesan cheese, grated

Dash of paprika

8 eggs

Sliced rustic bread, toasted, for serving

Handful of basil leaves, ripped by hand or roughly chopped

ITALIAN OMELETTE

Frittata   Serves 4

Whisk the eggs in a large mixing bowl and set aside.

Heat a large nonstick skillet over medium-low heat and add the olive oil. When it is hot, add the beaten eggs, salt, and pepper. When the eggs begin to set, sprinkle the green onions over the top.

Continue cooking, and as the eggs set, push their cooked edges toward the center of the pan using a spatula or wooden spoon, letting the uncooked eggs flow underneath. Be sure you don't scramble the eggs.

When the eggs are cooked (about 2 minutes), carefully flip the frittata in the pan so the browned side is up. Remove from heat, remove the frittata from the pan, and place it on a cutting board.

Spread the ricotta cheese on top and cover with sliced prosciutto. Drizzle with the extra-virgin olive oil and cut into 4 equal-size pieces for serving.

8 eggs

2 tbsp. olive oil

A pinch of salt and pepper

1 cup green onions, chopped

½ cup ricotta cheese, room temperature

8 thin slices prosciutto

1 tbsp. extra-virgin olive oil

TIP: To avoid scrambling the eggs, just move them a little bit—don't go ballistic!

PISSED OFF EGGS

Uova Incazzate

Serves 2

We couldn't afford much, but the way we used simple and inexpensive ingredients made them great. The eggs are called "pissed off" because we would make the dish in one clay pot for everyone. We would try to leave a corner without hot pepper for Grandma, but when the sauce is boiling and the oil bubbles, the spice gets everywhere. Grandma used to get really pissed because she loved the dish but she hated the heat.

Preheat the oven to broil.

Put the tomato sauce, crushed garlic, and sliced peppers in an oven-safe pan.

Crack the eggs into the pan and top with the red onion and garlic. Cover with the Parmesan cheese and drizzle with olive oil.

Place the pan under the broiler for 5–10 min, or until the cheese is golden brown and the eggs are cooked.

Remove the pan from the oven and use a spoon to push the basil leaves under the eggs, helping to separate the eggs from the pan. Drizzle again with extra-virgin olive oil.

Serve with crusty bread.

2 cups Fabio's Tomato Sauce (see recipe on page 18)

2 cloves garlic, crushed

4 fresh hot red chili peppers, thinly sliced

4 eggs

½ small red onion, thinly sliced

2 cloves garlic, thinly sliced

¼ cup Parmesan cheese, grated

Olive oil and extra-virgin olive oil, for drizzling

10–12 basil leaves

Crusty bread, for serving

STUFFED ZUCCHINI

Zucchini Ripiene   Serves 4

Preheat the oven to the highest broiler setting.

If using round zucchini, cut the tops off, scoop out the flesh with a spoon, and discard. If using long zucchini, cut them in half lengthwise and use a spoon to scoop out and discard the seeds.

Combine the cheeses, meats, and olives in a bowl and mix well. Fill the hollowed-out zucchini with the mixture, mounding the top. Drizzle with olive oil and place in an oven-safe pan.

Place the zucchini under the broiler, and broil for 10–12 minutes, until they are golden brown and crusty. Watch to make sure the cheese doesn't burn before the zucchini is cooked. If it starts to get too brown, cover the pan with aluminum foil to finish cooking.

Remove from heat, drizzle with extra-virgin olive oil, and serve.

4 zucchini (preferably the round ones called Eight Balls)

1 cup ricotta cheese

1 cup Parmesan cheese, grated

¼ lb. mortadella, chopped

¼ lb. Italian sausage crumbles, cooked (see note on page 201)

½ cup pitted black olives, chopped

Extra-virgin olive oil, for drizzling

PEPPER STEW

Peperonata   Serves 4–6

Heat the olive oil in a large pot over medium heat. Add the onion, garlic, and bay leaves and cook until the onion is golden brown.

Add the bell peppers, season with salt and pepper, and cook, stirring occasionally, until they begin to soften, about 10 minutes. Add the wine and the stock, increase the heat to high, bring to a boil, and cover with a lid. Turn the heat to low and simmer until the peppers are soft, about 20 minutes.

Add the capers and the basil and cook until the liquid has reduced to your preferred thickness.

½ cup olive oil

2 medium red onions, halved and sliced

8 cloves garlic, smashed

3 bay leaves

6 red bell peppers (or mixed colors), seeded and cut into 1-inch-wide slices

Salt and pepper

1 cup red wine

1 cup vegetable stock (see recipe on page 264)

2 tbsp. capers, drained, or rinsed if salted

½ bunch fresh basil, torn

FUNDAMENTALS & BREADS

Basi di Cucina

CH. **11**

You want spicy oil? Make your own! You want bread? Make your own! It's going to take more time for you to go buy your bread than to make it.

SOUR GRAPE SAUCE WITH ALMONDS

Sugo di Agresto   Makes 1½ cups

You have to be careful when you use this, because the flavor is very strong. It's best with grilled meat or fish with a bold flavor, as it can overwhelm lighter dishes. It's also great to serve with a cheese plate. When choosing your grapes, make sure to get a less sweet variety.

After removing the stems, soak the grapes in a bowl of cold water for 15 minutes.

Combine the grapes, shallots, parsley, capers, garlic, almonds, and walnuts with the oil in a small saucepan and cook for about 10 minutes over medium heat.

Soak the bread in the vinegar for 10 minutes. Very lightly squeeze the bread, leaving a lot of vinegar in it. Add the bread to the saucepan.

Set the saucepan over low heat and, stirring continuously, add the honey and season with salt and pepper. Cook for 10 minutes, adding the broth or water as needed to keep the sauce from drying out. When it's finished, the sauce should be rather thick.

Transfer the sauce to a crockery or glass bowl and let it cool completely before serving.

- 1 lb. seedless grapes, preferably red, cut in half
- 2 shallots, minced
- 1 bunch Italian parsley, leaves only
- 1 tbsp. capers, minced
- 2 cloves garlic, minced
- 1 cup blanched almonds, chopped
- 1 cup walnuts, chopped
- 2 tbsp. olive oil
- 2 cups white bread, crusts removed, chopped
- ½ cup red wine vinegar
- 3 tsp. honey
- Salt and pepper
- ½ cup water or beef stock (see recipe on page 263)

GREEN SAUCE WITH SIX HERBS AND HARD-BOILED EGGS

Salsa Verde

Makes 3 cups

This sauce is good with meat (see my mom's recipe for Boiled Meat on page 246) or with seafood such as mussels or a simple whitefish fillet. It's an herb sauce with a lot of oil and a lot of flavor but not a lot of calories—a perfect sauce when you're dieting. It will keep forever if you cover it with olive oil for storing.

Soak the bread in the vinegar for about 10 minutes, then squeeze it out.

In a food processor with the blade attachment, combine the cornichons, capers, anchovies, and all the herbs, and pulse until finely chopped but not a paste. Add the bread and the hard-boiled eggs and pulse 2 or 3 times.

Scrape down the sides of the bowl, add the oil, and pulse to combine.

2 slices white bread, crusts removed

⅓ cup white wine vinegar

8 cornichons or other small pickles

2 tsp. salt-packed capers, rinsed well

2–3 salt-packed anchovies, rinsed well and any bones removed

½ tbsp. fresh rosemary, roughly chopped

½ tbsp. fresh sage, roughly chopped

½ tbsp. fresh tarragon, roughly chopped

½ tbsp. fresh chives, roughly chopped

10 basil leaves

2 hard-boiled eggs, roughly chopped

2 cups extra-virgin olive oil

BABY ONION SAUCE

Salsa di Cipolline

Makes 3 cups

This is good for anything pork and for anything braised. Onions have different degrees of intensity—from green onions to sweet onions to pearl onions to red onions to yellow onions. You can use whatever onions you like best. This is a guideline that will help you through the making of an onion sauce, rather than tell you exactly what you have to do. Make sense?

Put the onions, olive oil, and some salt and pepper in a Dutch oven and cook over medium heat for about 35 minutes. The onions should be caramelized and still whole.

Add the stock, rosemary, brown sugar, and lemon juice, and reduce until the juice has disappeared, the onions are falling apart, and the sauce has thickened.

Add the mint and let the sauce cool down. Store it covered with olive oil in an airtight container in the fridge. It will keep for 2 weeks.

2 lb. pearl onions, peeled, rinsed, and patted dry

4 tbsp. olive oil

Salt and pepper

1 cup vegetable stock (see recipe on page 264)

2 tbsp. fresh rosemary, minced

1 tbsp. brown sugar

Juice of 3 lemons

10–15 small mint leaves

TIP: Hear me out, please! Go read about common sense on caramelization on page 4 of the Introduction.

BÉCHAMEL SAUCE

Besciamella

Melt the butter in a deep saucepan over medium heat. Reduce heat to low, and slowly mix in the flour. Add the nutmeg and stir.

    Remove from heat and slowly add the milk, stirring continuously. Return to heat and bring the sauce to a boil, continuing to stir.

    When the sauce has thickened and will coat the back of a spoon, season with salt and pepper.

    Turn off the heat and let the sauce rest for 30 minutes before using.

8 tbsp. (1 stick) butter
¼ cup flour
1 tsp. nutmeg
4 cups milk
Salt and pepper

BALSAMIC GLAZE

Aceto Balsamico Ridotto

This is the way we cheat when we can't afford to buy aged balsamic vinegar. Instead of waiting twenty-five years, you only have to wait four to five hours, so you can get dinner made before your newborn child graduates from college.

Combine the vinegar and molasses or honey in a pot and bring to a boil. Reduce to about 1 1/2 cups total and remove from the heat to cool.

    Put the vinegar in a squeeze bottle and use it cold.

4 cups balsamic vinegar
1 cup molasses or light
  honey

TUSCAN FRUIT MUSTARD

Mostarda Toscano

This is delicious eaten with cheese.

Pulse the grapes in a food processor, then strain the pulp through a fine-mesh colander to collect the juices. Discard the pulp.

In a stockpot, combine the pears and apples with the honey, mustard, Vin Santo wine, and clove. Cover and cook over low heat until all the liquid has evaporated and the fruit is very soft.

In a separate saucepan, boil the grape juice with the mustard seeds, then simmer for about 20 minutes, until it has reduced by half. Strain the liquid again, discarding the mustard seeds and, while it is still very hot, add it to the stockpot with the fruit.

Cook the fruit for 5 minutes more, mashing any remaining pulp. Cool completely, add the lemon zest, and stir to combine. Then transfer the mustard to a glass mason jar.

3 lb. very ripe and sweet seedless white or red grapes, stem discarded

4 ripe pears, peeled and cut into cubes

3 sour green apples, peeled and cut into cubes

3 tbsp. honey

1 generous tsp. yellow mustard

1 cup Vin Santo (or any sweet wine that is not sparkling)

1 whole clove

2 tbsp. hot mustard seeds, crushed

Zest of 2 lemons

TIP: Change the fruit for your mustard base depending upon the season.

MAYONNAISE WITH VARIATIONS

FUNDAMENTALS
& BREADS

Maionese

Makes about 2 cups

Who doesn't adore mayonnaise? It's a great spread, and it's nice in pasta salad or in a dressing. The problem with the mayonnaise you buy is that in order to be shelf stable for six months, it has to be filled with a whole bunch of additives, preservatives, conservatives, coloring agents . . . Real mayonnaise contains nothing bad for you. It's only egg, a little bit of oil, a few drops of lemon, and a touch of salt and pepper. So make your own.

2 egg yolks

1½ to 2 cups olive oil

½ tsp. fine salt

½ tsp. white pepper

2 tsp. fresh-squeezed lemon juice

Place the egg yolks in a food processor and turn it on, letting the yolks run alone for about 1 minute. Then add 1 cup of oil in a very thin stream. As you do, the yolks will start to become whiter and fluffier.

Add the salt and pulse 5 times, then add pepper and keep pulsing. When the salt and pepper are incorporated, add 2 tablespoons of lemon juice and turn the food processor on again. Add another ½ cup of oil in a very thin stream, alternating with the remaining 2 tablespoons of lemon juice.

Stop the food processor and check the consistency of the mayonnaise with your finger. If it's really thick, stop here. If it's still runny, turn the food processor back on and add the remaining ½ cup of oil, again in a very thin stream.

TIP: To cook right, you have to look at your food!

VARIATIONS:

After you have made the basic mayonnaise, add one of these ingredients (or one of your own). If the mayonnaise looks too liquid after your addition, incorporate more olive oil.

The mayonnaise will keep until the expiration date of the eggs you used to make it.

5–6 sundried tomatoes

1 tbsp. pesto

Your favorite mixed herbs (or whatever you have)

FABIO'S MOM'S CRÈME FRAÎCHE

Renza Panna Acida

Whisk together the cream, buttermilk, and lemon juice, and place the mixture in a jar or container with a cloth or cheesecloth fastened tightly over the top.

Let it rest for 18–24 hours at room temperature, until it is a bit firmer than heavy cream, almost like yogurt. Enjoy it right away or cover with a lid and refrigerate up to a week.

2 cups heavy cream

1 tbsp. buttermilk

½ tsp. lemon juice

LEMON DRESSING

Condimento al Limone

If for special health reasons, you are concerned about raw eggs, you can buy pasteurized egg yolks.

Mix all the ingredients well in a blender at high speed. Strain the dressing and store it in an airtight container in the refrigerator. Shake well before using.

⅓ cup extra-virgin olive oil

4 tbsp. lemon juice

1½ tbsp. mint leaves, chopped

Zest of 1 lemon

3 egg yolks

Salt and pepper

BALSAMIC VINAIGRETTE

Condimento al Balsamico

Makes ¾ cup

Reduce the vinegar by half in a small pot over medium heat.

Mix the reduced vinegar with all the other ingredients except the Parmesan in a blender at high speed, blending until the dressing is smooth. Strain out the shallot, add the Parmesan, and mix well.

Store in an airtight container in the refrigerator. Shake well before using.

½ cup balsamic vinegar

⅓ cup extra-virgin olive oil

1 shallot, finely minced

1 tsp. white sugar

A pinch of black pepper

¼ cup Parmesan cheese, grated

ITALIAN DRESSING

Condimento Italiano

Makes ½ cup dry mix, 1 cup dressing

Combine the parsley with all the dry seasoning-mix ingredients. Store in an airtight container. It will keep for about a month on the shelf or in the fridge for about 3 months.

To make the dressing, add 2 tablespoons of seasoning mix and one tablespoon of sugar to ⅓ cup vinegar and ⅔ cup extra-virgin olive oil. Shake well or whisk together in a bowl.

For the seasoning mix:

1 tbsp. fresh parsley, finely chopped

1 tbsp. garlic salt

1 tbsp. onion powder

1 tbsp. rosemary, finely chopped (fresh is better, but dry is fine)

2 tbsp. dried oregano

1 tsp. pepper

¼ tsp. dried thyme

1 tsp. dried basil

¼ tsp. celery salt

2 tbsp. salt

For the dressing:

1 tbsp. sugar

⅓ cup balsamic vinegar (or red wine if you prefer)

⅔ cup extra-virgin olive oil

INFUSED FLAVORED OIL

Olio Truccato

Makes 3 cups

This can also be made with tarragon, rosemary, sage, or fennel fronds.

Bring a pot of water to a medium boil and add the baking soda. While you are waiting, prepare an ice bath in a large bowl and set it aside (see note on page 196 for how to make an ice bath).

Put the basil in the boiling water and count 45 seconds. The basil should be barely wilted. Take it out and plunge it into the ice bath immediately to preserve its color. After about 10 seconds, remove it and drain, squeezing the leaves well. (You can also pat it dry with a towel.)

Put the basil and the oil in a blender at high speed for at least 30 seconds. Transfer the mixture into a saucepan over medium heat and cook for about 2 minutes, just enough to barely heat it.

Pour the oil through a fine-mesh strainer into a glass jar (it's okay if some of the basil pulp goes into the oil). Once it has cooled, transfer the oil to a bottle with a pouring lid. It will keep in the fridge for as long as it takes you to use it up!

1 tsp. baking soda
4 cups tightly packed fresh
   basil leaves
3 cups extra-virgin olive oil

DRIED BREADCRUMBS

Pangrattato

If you dry the bread outside the window like we used to at my house, make sure to check for bird droppings! Remove the piece of bread hit by the bird and discard.

Cut the bread into cubes about 1 inch wide.

Spread the cubes on trays and let them air-dry for several days, until the bread is very dry. You may need to heat the cubes in a 200°F oven for 1–2 hours to reduce the moisture. If you do this, let the bread cool completely before you grind it.

Working in batches, place the bread cubes mixed with the herbs in a food processor and pulse until the bread is reduced to fine crumbs.

Use right away or store in freezer bags to keep the crumbs fresh. You can freeze them for up to 1 month.

2 loaves stale bread (the best choice is whatever is left over!)

2 tsp. dried rosemary

2 tsp. dried sage

ARBORIO RICE COATING

Farina di Riso

Makes 7 cups

Grind the rice in a blender until very fine, then combine in a bowl with the flour, the semolina flour, and the salt and pepper. Toss until well blended. Store the coating in a tightly sealed container in the freezer for maximum freshness. Use it instead of bread crumbs for frying whenever you want an extra-crunchy outside.

3 cups Arborio rice
3 cups unbleached flour
1 cup semolina flour
2 tbsp. salt
2 tsp. pepper

AROMATIC FLAVORED SALT

Sale Truccato

Makes 2 cups

Using either a food processor or a mortar and pestle, combine all the ingredients.

Store in an airtight container in the refrigerator and use for seasoning all kinds of meat and fish.

2 cups salt
2 tbsp. garlic powder
3 tbsp. fresh rosemary, minced
4 juniper berries
3 sage leaves
1 tbsp. fennel seeds

CHICKPEA BREAD

Cecina

Serves 6–8

Preheat the oven to 375°F.

In the bowl of a stand mixer with a hook attachment, combine the water, 2 tablespoons of the oil, and the flour or pulverized chickpeas. Then add a pinch of salt, the baking powder, and the garlic powder. Keep mixing for about 5 minutes, until the batter looks like a thick paste. It's important that lumps don't form; if they do, dissolve them with a whisk.

Cover the bowl with a moist towel and let it rest in a cool place for about 45 minutes.

Pour the remaining 2 tablespoons of oil into a large (about 14-inch) baking dish lined with parchment paper and spread it to cover the entire dish. Without shaking the dish, pour in the batter so that it floats on top of the oil. Bake for 40–45 minutes or longer, until a thin golden crust forms. Serve hot with a drizzle of oil and freshly ground pepper.

6 cups cold water

4 tbsp. olive oil

1½ lb. chickpea flour or dry chickpeas pulverized in a blender

Salt and pepper

1 tsp. baking powder

1 tsp. garlic powder

Piadina

Everyone in Italy loves to make their own bread, and piadina is just one kind of good homemade flatbread. It's really quick to make, and doesn't make a mess.

Combine the flour, baking soda, and salt and pepper in a stand mixer equipped with the dough hook attachment. Mix for a few minutes to ensure that all the dry ingredients are well combined. Add the butter and mix on low speed until it is incorporated.

Slowly add up to 2/3 cup water, about a teaspoon every few minutes, until the mixture forms dough around the hook. Keep kneading on the lowest speed for about 5–6 minutes.

Transfer the dough to a lightly floured work surface and cut it into 5 equal pieces. Wrap each piece in plastic wrap and refrigerate for 30 minutes.

When the dough has chilled, roll each ball out into a disc about 5–6 inches across and about 1 inch thick (try to keep it round!).

Now you can grill them or bake them in the oven at 375°F until the tops are lightly browned. Brush the tops with extra-virgin olive oil and sprinkle with coarse salt.

4 cups flour, plus more for dusting

3 tsp. baking soda

Sea salt and white pepper

2/3 cup butter

2/3 cup water

3 tbsp. extra-virgin olive oil

Coarse salt

TIP: Piadina is also delicious as pita chips if you cut it and leave it in the oven a bit longer.

BREAD FOR SICK PEOPLE

Pane dei Malati

Whole wheat flour has a lot of iron and protein in it, so whole wheat bread is the only kind you get when you're in the hospital in Italy. People make it at home, too, of course, because it's delicious. The recurring joke in my family was whenever my mom would make bread with whole wheat flour, we'd tease her and say: "What? Am I sick?"

Prepare the starter: Mix all the ingredients except the 2 tablespoons of flour in a bowl. Once it is well mixed and the yeast has dissolved, sprinkle the remaining flour over the starter. Cover the bowl with a cotton towel and let it rest in a warm place for about an hour, until the starter has doubled in size (the top flour will disappear).

When the starter is ready, place it into a stand mixer with the hook attachment and add the whole wheat flour, the salt, and the milk. Then add the cup of flour little by little while mixing continuously. At this point you should have a mass that you can handle easily.

Sprinkle the remaining 1/4 cup of flour onto a wooden cutting board and knead the dough with the palms of your hands, in a folding motion, for 5 minutes.

Heavily flour a cotton towel. Shape the dough into a 12-inch loaf and place it in the prepared towel. Wrap the towel all around the loaf and set it aside until it has increased in size by about half (45 minutes to an hour). While it is rising, preheat the oven to 400°F (or 375°F if using a convection oven).

Bake for about 1 hour, or until the crust is crisp and brown and the bread sounds hollow when you tap the crust.

For the starter:

1½ cups plus 2 tbsp. flour
1 oz. fresh compressed yeast or 2 packages active dry yeast
1 cup water, lukewarm
1 tsp. salt

For the dough:

2 cups whole wheat flour
A pinch of salt
1 cup whole milk, lukewarm
1 cup plus ¼ cup flour

OLIVE BREAD

Pane alle Olive

Makes 1 loaf

Mix the olives and the oil together in a small bowl.

Prepare the starter: Place 4 tablespoons of the flour in a small bowl and make a well in the center. Dissolve the yeast in the warm water and place the mixture, along with the salt, into the well. Mix thoroughly, then dust the remaining tablespoon of flour over the starter. Cover the bowl with a cotton towel and let it rest in a warm place for about an hour until it has doubled in size (the top flour will disappear).

When the starter is ready, place it, the olives, and all the remaining ingredients except the flour into the bowl of a stand mixer. Using the hook attachment, mix the dough at medium speed, adding the 6 cups of flour a little at a time until it is all incorporated. You should have a ball of dough that is not sticky to the touch.

Shape the dough into a loaf, cover it completely with a very well-floured towel, and let it rest in a warm place until it has doubled in size. While it is rising, preheat the oven to 375°F.

Place the loaf of dough onto a floured sheet pan and onto the middle or lower rack of the oven. Bake for about 2 hours or until it sounds dry and hollow when you tap the crust. Remove from the oven and let it rest for about 2 hours on a cooling rack.

3 cups mixed olives, pitted
   and chopped

1 tbsp. extra-virgin olive oil

For the starter:

5 heaping tbsp. unbleached
   flour

3 oz. fresh compressed
   yeast or 6 packages
   active dry yeast

1 cup water, lukewarm

A pinch of salt

For the dough:

1 cup water, lukewarm

2 tsp. salt

1 tsp. pepper

6 cups unbleached flour,
   plus more for the pan.

I think except for seeing the birth of your first child and the first time you make love to somebody, the biggest emotion possible is when you break a loaf of bread that you made on your own.

TUSCAN BREAD

Pane Toscano   Makes 1 loaf

I think except for seeing the birth of your first child and the first time you make love to somebody, the biggest emotion possible is when you break a loaf of bread that you made on your own. It's like being the first man on the moon, and it happens every time.

Prepare the starter: In a glass or ceramic bowl, dissolve the yeast in the water. Add the flour and the salt, mix well with a wooden spoon, add the pepper, and let rest 5 minutes. Sprinkle with the remaining tablespoon of flour. Cover the bowl with a cotton towel and let it rest in a warm place for about an hour, until the starter has doubled in size (the top flour will disappear).

When the starter is ready, place it into a stand mixer with the hook attachment and add 4 cups of the flour and half of the water. When it is all incorporated, add the remaining water, mix it in, and use the remaining flour to detach the dough from the bowl and dust your hands and a work surface. Knead the dough with the palms of your hands, in a folding motion, for 5 minutes.

Shape the loaf in the way you like it. Traditionally it is round, but you can do a football shape, too. Mark the top with a knife, making a few incisions less than 1/4-inch deep. Wrap the dough in a towel and let it rest in a warm place until it has doubled in size (about an hour). While it is rising, preheat the oven to 400°F (or 375°F if using a convection oven).

When the dough is ready, quickly unfold the towel and place the dough directly onto a baking sheet and into the oven. Bake the bread for about 55 minutes, until it sounds hollow when you tap the crust. Do not open the oven for the first 30 minutes of baking time.

Let the bread cool on a rack before serving.

For the starter:

1 oz. fresh compressed yeast or 2 packages active dry yeast

½ cup water, lukewarm

¾ cup plus 1 tbsp. flour

Salt and pepper

For the dough:

5 cups unbleached flour

1¾ cups water, lukewarm

One of the only things I know for sure is that I've always been chasing something: a better meal on the table, more money for my family, the next great thing. I keep chasing after dreams because, as my mom wrote to me when I came to the United States, nothing else makes me happy. I've failed many times, but I've also learned that in life, it doesn't matter how many times people try to push you down. You've just got to be willing to get up again.

As for my life in America, I am blessed. The biggest lesson I've learned here is that it doesn't matter how rich you are, how rich your parents are, what kind of studies you did, or how good the school you attended was. Those things can influence the outcome a little bit. But what really matters is not how good you are or how good you've had it, it's only how badly you want it. If you want it badly enough, nothing else matters. Nothing will ever be in your way. Not your past, your present, not what happened or will happen. You'll find a way to succeed.

But you have to know who you are. I know that you can take me out of Italy, but you will never take Italy out of me. One thing my mom always told me was, "Fabio, I know you will be successful. But never forget where you come from. Because if you forget where you come from, you'll be a successful but empty person. If

If you want it badly enough, nothing else matters. Nothing will ever be in your way. Not your past, your present, not what happened or will happen.

you are grateful and appreciate every day, you'll be joyful. You were always so happy even when we had nothing, so remember: America is a great country for opportunities. But happiness is not measured by what you have, but by how much you appreciate it."

So, even though I may get beat up with a wooden spoon because of this book, since people in Italy don't share traditional recipes except with family members (and even then usually only with the women), it's very important to me because these stories and recipes tell you who I am. There are about fifty more dishes I wish I could share with you, but I can't because my great-grandma took those secrets with her when she died. Only she knows how many capers you need or how much oil. For those meals, you'll have to go to heaven and meet her. I'm sure she'll be happy to cook for you there. For now, enjoy her cooking here, through this book. *Buon appetito.*

ACKNOWLEDGMENTS

I would really like to thank the people at Hyperion, not only for publishing my book but for setting the bar so high for any other book to come. Ellen Archer, thank you for trusting this crazy, passionate, Italian nutcase. To my editor, Elisabeth Dyssegaard; her assistant, Samantha O'Brien; Shubhani Sarkar, who designed the book; David Lott, who handled production; Betsy Hulsebosch in marketing; and Christine Ragasa, Kristina Miller, and Kathryn Hough in publicity; you all helped make *Fabio's Italian Kitchen* what it is, which is a reflection of all the things I love most about food and cooking and, of course, Italy. I love you guys, thank you for bringing me in. Melanie Rehak translated my messed-up English into something readable by anyone in the United States, or anyone who speaks English anywhere. Without her, you wouldn't even be able to use this book. Thanks to Matt Armendariz for taking amazing pictures of my food. We did ten to fifteen dishes a day and he's a rock star. I want to thank my wonderful kitchen staff, John Paolone and Jonathan Lynch, for helping me prep all the dishes in the book. No food stylist is necessary when you have those two! Guys, without you I wouldn't be able to do everything I do. I'm very thankful for your friendship and for all the hard work you do every day. I want to thank my family, of course, and God for the faith I have. I also want to thank God for dealing with and putting up with my grandma and grandpa every day. I know they can be pains when it comes to food, but hey—you're God so I know you can handle it! To the magnificent #teamfabio—this book is for you, too. You rock my kitchen every single day. To everyone who tried—and sometimes succeeded—in making my life harder, or who tried to take advantage of me in one way or another, this book is more proof that you only made me stronger and wiser. Now I'm bulletproof. Finally, I would like to thank everybody in the United States who is aware of who I am—my friends, my fans, and so many other people. Without each and every one of you guys this would not have been possible. I'm very honored and very blessed to be in the position I'm in today. From the bottom of my Italian heart, thank you.

31901051959304